The
Reference Shelf ®

Democracy Evolving

The Reference Shelf
Volume 91 • Number 4
H.W. Wilson
A Division of EBSCO Information Services, Inc.

Published by
GREY HOUSE PUBLISHING
Amenia, New York
2019

The Reference Shelf

The books in this series contain reprints of articles, excerpts from books, addresses on current issues, and studies of social trends in the United States and other countries. There are six separately bound numbers in each volume, all of which are usually published in the same calendar year. Numbers one through five are each devoted to a single subject, providing background information and discussion from various points of view and concluding with an index and comprehensive bibliography that lists books, pamphlets, and articles on the subject. The final number of each volume is a collection of recent speeches. Books in the series may be purchased individually or on subscription.

Publisher's Cataloging-In-Publication Data
(Prepared by The Donohue Group, Inc.)

Names: Grey House Publishing, Inc., compiler.
Title: Democracy evolving / [compiled by Grey House Publishing].
Other Titles: Reference shelf ; v. 91, no. 4.
Description: Amenia, New York : Grey House Publishing, 2019. | Includes bibliographical references and index.
Identifiers: ISBN 9781642652215 (v. 91, no. 4) | ISBN 9781642652178 (volume set)
Subjects: LCSH: Democracy--United States--History. | United States--Politics and government. | Patriotism--United States--History.
Classification: LCC JK1726 .D46 2019 | DDC 320.973--dc23

Printed in Canada

Contents

3

Democracy or Dictatorship?

4

How Fragile is Democracy?

5

What Do We Think of Democracy?

Preface

The Changing Face of Democracy

A majority of Americans are worried about the state of American democracy. Political and social scientists have found, in their studies of Americans' attitudes about pride of country, that the United States may be in a state of democratic crisis. The reasons are complex, and include a loss of legitimacy in America's electoral system, deepening frustration with government's inability to address income inequality and institutionalized racism, and generational shifts in values. In 2001, before the 9/11 terrorist attacks, a Gallup poll found that 55 percent of Americans were "extremely proud" to be American. After surging to between 65 and 70 percent after 9/11, levels began to drop after the invasion of Iraq did not produce the desired results. The highly divisive political and social climate of America in the twenty-first century—arguably exacerbated by the election of the polarizing Donald Trump—has resulted in an unprecedented plunge in pride of country. In 2018, for the first time, less than half of Americans reported being proud of the United States. While patriotic sentiment fell among white people, the dip was even more pronounced among people of color, with just over 30 percent reporting a strong sense of "American pride."[1] Whether or not there is a democratic crisis, and what is causing it, is a subject of intense debate. However, the fact that more than half of Americans perceive America's democratic system as failing indicates a legitimate problem.

Democracy and Its Alternatives

American society is a representative democracy, a system in which the people elect representatives who then participate in the process of making and amending laws. Our democratic system was carefully constructed to be resistant to authoritarianism by a complex system of checks and balances to prevent tyranny. Over the centuries, Americans and their representatives have engaged in an effort to refine America's government to expand the benefits of citizenship to the greatest number of people possible.

But unforeseen problems have also arisen, leading to what some view as a shift away from the framers' original intentions. One trend has been a concentration of power in the executive branch. While historians believe that the framers intended Congress to be the most powerful of the three branches, there is evidence that a gridlocked party system and continuing delegation of authority to the executive branch have significantly weakened Congress. And, the Supreme Court has often been unwilling to intervene because of a lack of clearly defined executive boundaries in the Constitution.[2] Congress is made up of individuals from different parties reflecting differing viewpoints on issues, while the presidency represents one party. As a result, this increased authority in the executive branch means that the will of the people, as expressed through their elected Congressional representatives, is less accurately reflected. Political scientist Yascha Mounk says that Americans' democratic participation has "miniscule, near-zero, statistically non-significant impact on public policy." Mounk envisions the current system as one that violates constitutional principles through voting manipulation and misinformation campaigns.[3]

Changes in society have had a profound impact on democracy as well. The most hopeful view of the Digital Age was that the internet and social media would increase political participation and civic engagement, reaching an unprecedented number of people. Some contend, however, that an unintended consequence of the Digital Age is increased polarization. Georgetown University Professor Joshua A. Geltzer calls this "hyper-democratization," or a "shift away from the mediate, checked republic that America's founders carefully crafted." He says, "We're increasingly ruled by an online mob. And it's a mob getting besieged with misinformation."[4]

The spread of social media in politics has also left Americans vulnerable to targeted misinformation campaigns. A prominent recent example is the Russian election interference scandal of 2016, when Russian intelligence operatives disseminated false information with the following goals: to support the election of Donald Trump; to destabilize American society; to make the U.S. government less effective internationally; and to reduce the possibility of action against Russia under an alternative president, i.e. Hillary Clinton. Though the Trump administration has downplayed this incident, many Americans saw it as undermining the integrity of American democracy.[5]

The current administration has also been accused of utilizing authoritarian tactics to control the information environment, particularly by referring to mainstream news outlets as "fake news." Republican Senator Jeff Flake of Arizona criticized Trump's actions regarding mainstream media:

> 2017 was a year which saw the truth—objective, empirical, evidence-based truth—more battered and abused than any other in the history of our country, at the hands of the most powerful figure in our government. It was a year which saw the White House enshrine "alternative facts" into the American lexicon, as justification for what used to be known simply as good old-fashioned falsehoods. It was the year in which an unrelenting daily assault on the constitutionally protected free press was launched by that same White House, an assault that is as unprecedented as it is unwarranted. "The enemy of the people," was what the president of the United States called the free press in 2017.
>
> Mr. President, it is a testament to the condition of our democracy that our own president uses words infamously spoken by Josef Stalin to describe his enemies. It bears noting that so fraught with malice was the phrase "enemy of the people," that even

Nikita Khrushchev forbade its use, telling the Soviet Communist Party that the phrase had been introduced by Stalin for the purpose of "annihilating such individuals" who disagreed with the supreme leader.[6]

Today's digital environment has also seen the birth of an industry in which individuals earn profits for creating fake news based on the number of times that internet users "click" through their post or article, encouraging the invention of highly sensationalized and often false claims. The inability of many Americans to differentiate between willful manipulation and fake media content, coupled with a movement away from legitimate news, has resulted in more Americans developing skewed and potentially dangerous views. The infamous Comet Ping Pong pizza incident, in which fake news influenced a man to travel to Washington D.C. armed with an assault rifle to free children from a child trafficking ring allegedly led by Hillary Clinton, is one example of a situation in which the erosion of trust in information nearly led to violence.

The free press is a cornerstone of any true democracy because it is through the press that the people access information from experts, evaluate the claims of politicians and pundits, and inform themselves to take part in the democratic process. The health of any democracy is equated to the degree to which citizens participate, and the degree to which they have access to legitimate information. Current attacks on America's media and information environment have no doubt encouraged the perception that American democracy is in decay.

The challenges currently faced by democracy have impacted attitudes about it. In October of 2017, Pew Research found a shift away from democratic ideals in some of the world's bastions of democratic government and an increasing interest in alternative forms of government, the very thing that the framers were aiming to prevent. Also, a large percentage of Americans and those in other democracies demonstrated interest in exploring radical departures from representative democracy, believing that nations would be better governed by experts in the sciences and other fields than by elected politicians, a belief tied to the growing international perception that elected leaders have been ineffective at dealing with the world's most pressing problems. Pew Research found that 40 percent of Americans hold favorable views of a system in which experts, rather than professional politicians, decide how best to manage the country. Similarly, in America and other democracies, an increasing share of people expressed support for a shift away from representative democracy toward direct democracy. In this most basic and earliest form of democracy, people, rather than elected representatives, vote directly on policy proposals.[7]

The 2018 election of New York Representative Alexandria Ocasio-Cortez and the 2016 and 2020 presidential campaigns of Bernie Sanders have stimulated interest in democratic socialism, a system of government that blends socialist and democratic principles and focuses on utilizing the government as a force for equalization and social welfare. Ideals such as socialized healthcare and higher education have captivated millions of Americans frustrated with the rising costs of even basic services in the United States. Whereas expressing support for socialism was once considered taboo in America, many Americans—especially younger Americans—are warming to the idea and this may play an important role in the future of American policy.[8]

Economic Roots of the Conflict

The willingness of Americans to look for more extreme solutions—like direct democracy, democratic socialism, and even authoritarianism—to the country's perennial problems reflect their growing insecurity about the American economic system and quality of life. Though it was once widely accepted that American democracy and capitalism were necessary to one another, the advance of China's economy, a semi-free-market system existing within an otherwise authoritarian regime, questions whether the democratic system is necessary or helpful in addressing America's economic challenges.

America's particular form of free-market capitalism is dominated by conservative attitudes regarding economic regulation, enabling corporations and wealthy individuals to concentrate wealth. Even as Americans at every level of the economy participate in the growth of the economy and the rise in productivity, few reap the rewards. Income and wealth inequality in 2019 are at the highest levels since just before the turn of the last century, likely one of the reasons for the uptick in political activism and why more Americans are demonstrating interest in radical solutions.[9]

A Matter of Perception

America's democratic system can be said to be working if most, if not all, Americans have faith and trust in the system; when a majority lack this faith, the system is failing. Politicians and political scientists have identified many areas of concern in America's political environment, but less clear are the solutions that might be utilized to restore America's democratic institutions or American faith in the system. At the founding of the American experiment, the framers envisioned an agile, changeable governmental system that could withstand the test of time and adapt to changing social and cultural realities. An evolution of America's governmental system may demonstrate that the democratic system itself can be changed without sacrificing the most fundamental value of America—government by *and* for the people.

Works Used

Geltzer, Joshua. "America's Problem Isn't Too Little Democracy: It's Too Much." *Politico Magazine*. June 26, 2018. Retrieved from https://www.politico.com/magazine/story/2018/06/26/america-democracy-trump-russia-2016-218894.

"Income Inequality." *Pew Research Center*. May 7, 2019. Retrieved from https://www.pewresearch.org/topics/income-inequality/.

Mohdin, Aamna. "Fewer Than Half of Americans Are 'Extremely Proud' of Their Country." *QZ*. Jul 4, 2018. Retrieved from https://qz.com/1321228/fewer-than-half-of-americans-are-extremely-proud-of-their-country-for-the-first-time-in-18-years-gallup/.

Mounk, Yascha. "America Is Not a Democracy." *The Atlantic*. March 2018. Retrieved from https://www.theatlantic.com/magazine/archive/2018/03/america-is-not-a-democracy/550931/.

"Read Sen. Jeff Flake's Speech Criticizing Trump." *CNN*. Jan 17, 2018. Retrieved from https://www.cnn.com/2018/01/17/politics/jeff-flake-speech/index.html.

Stiglitz, Joseph E. "A 'Democratic Socialist' Agenda Is Appealing: No Wonder Trump Attacks It." *The Washington Post*. May 8, 2019. Retrieved from https://www.washingtonpost.com/opinions/a-democratic-socialist-agenda-is-appealing-no-wonder-trump-attacks-it/2019/05/08/f3db9e42-71a2-11e9-9eb4-0828f5389013_story.html?utm_term=.3cce33a1d2de.

Todd, Chuck, Murray, Mark, and Carrie Dann. "Russian Interference Is the Red Flag from Mueller That Everyone Is Missing." *NBC News*. May 30, 2019. Retrieved from https://www.nbcnews.com/politics/meet-the-press/russian-interference-red-flag-mueller-everyone-missing-n1011866.

White, Adam J. "Democracy, Delegation, and Distrust." The Hoover Institute. Mar 12, 2019. Retrieved from https://www.hoover.org/research/democracy-delegation-and-distrust.

Wike, Richard, Simmons, Katie, Stokes, Bruce, and Janell Fetterolf. "Democracy Widely Supported, Little Backing for Rule by Strong Leader or Military." *Pew Research Center*. Oct 16, 2017. Retrieved from https://www.pewresearch.org/global/2017/10/16/democracy-widely-supported-little-backing-for-rule-by-strong-leader-or-military/.

Notes

1. Mohdin, "Fewer Than Half of Americans Are 'Extremely Proud' of Their Country."
2. White, "Democracy, Delegation, and Distrust."
3. Mounk, "America Is Not a Democracy."
4. Geltzer, "America's Problem Isn't Too Little Democracy: It's Too Much."
5. Todd, Murray, and Dann, "Russian Interference Is the Red Flag from Mueller That Everyone Is Missing."
6. "Read Sen. Jeff Flake's Speech Criticizing Trump," *CNN*.
7. Wike, Simmons, Stokes, and Fetterolf, "Democracy Widely Supported, Little Backing for Rule by Strong Leader or Military."
8. Stiglitz, "A 'Democratic Socialist' Agenda Is Appealing: No Wonder Trump Attacks It."
9. "Income Inequality." *Pew Research Center*.

1
Democracy Defined

While the United States is a representative democracy, Switzerland is a modern example of a direct democracy. Above, Swiss citizens attend a 2009 Landsgemeinde, or "canton assembly"—a public, non-secret ballot voting system—in 2009 in the canton of Glarus.

1

Democracy Defined

What Is American Democracy?

Is American democracy unique? The answer to this question depends on one's perspective. Though some believe that America is the birthplace of democracy, American democracy can best be thought of as an amalgamation of political and philosophical ideas from a variety of sources. These ideas were put together in such a way as to avoid the failings of Europe's authoritarian monarchies. Academics and political scientists from around the world have theorized that, in the twenty-first century, American democracy may be in peril. A loss of popular faith in the government, related in part to the inherent stagnation of America's adversarial two-party system, has led to a situation in which few Americans feel adequately represented. This is to some degree a function of America's democratic history, which prioritized limiting governmental power over fostering a cooperative system in which governmental function necessitated compromise and moderation.[1]

Constructing American Democracy

A democracy is any form of government in which the political power is seen as originating with the people. The simplest form of democracy is direct democracy, in which citizens of the state create and vote directly on laws and policies. The Athenian democracy of ancient Greece is the best-known historical example of this; all free male citizens were empowered to create and vote on the laws of the state. In Athens, the direct democratic approach was taken to such an extreme that citizens even voted on the outcome of court cases.[2] The nation of Switzerland is a primary example of a twenty-first century direct democracy. All Swiss citizens over the age of 18 are able to propose and vote on policy through public referenda. The direct system provides the simplest and most direct route for each citizen to see his or her own view on their country represented in the law, but political scientists generally believe that direct democracy is most effective when a population is small and relatively homogenous, as has been the case in Switzerland until recently.[3]

When debating the formation of America's democracy, the framers rejected direct democracy for several reasons. Direct democratic systems work best when the largest number of citizens participate and when a majority are informed enough to participate intelligently. When participation wanes, or when a large share of the population lack the information needed to contribute meaningfully to the process, direct democracy can lead to a state's laws originating from a small minority. It is often believed that direct democracies tend to stagnate when the population cannot agree on major issues, and critics of this form of government argue that there must be a system in place to essentially "break ties" and keep the government moving forward.

Thus, the framers of the United States chose a representative democracy, which is one in which the people elect representatives to make and change laws, in most cases without further direct input from citizens. At the time of America's establishment, most of the population were farmers or laborers with little formal education and little interest in the legal issues involved in forming America's political system. Under the representative system, individuals need not be cut out of the process entirely but could still play a role by making the far more basic decision to vote for certain candidates or align with a political party or group. A single vote cast for a candidate or party becomes dozens or even hundreds of votes cast by those elected representatives. On the most basic level, representative democracy is a simplified political system in which the only requirement for participation is that citizens choose between people or broad political philosophies, while the remaining function of government is handled without the need for direct public participation.

It is often argued that America is not really a democracy but a republic. This distinction has little importance as a republic—a system of government in which supreme power is vested in the people and executive power is vested in an elected representative—can be viewed as a type of representative democracy. The Founding Fathers debated republicanism versus democracy, but such debates were generally meant to differentiate the representative American system from the direct democracy of ancient Athens and of some European societies today, which the Founding Fathers sometimes referred to simply as a "democracy." Thus, when Americans argue about whether America is a democracy or a republic, generally the debate is a "pure" or "direct" democracy vs. a representative one.[4]

Representation or Marginalization?

One of the primary aims in establishing the American democratic system was to avoid the shortfalls of the European monarchies, in which families of aristocrats wielded absolute power and subjected their populations to what the founders typically described as "tyranny." In establishing the constitutional rules for American government, steps were taken to ensure that no single individual could wield sufficient power to become a tyrant. This took the form of "checks and balances" between the three branches of the American government: the legislature, the executive, and the judicial. For such a system to become tyrannical, an individual or group would need to control all three branches of government simultaneously. In America, this would mean that a single party controlled the presidency, both houses of Congress, and the judiciary, a situation that is extremely unlikely given term limits, local election systems, and other measures. However, if a single political group controls two branches of government, such as the presidency and Congress, the development of policy can become increasingly lopsided.

While the Constitution provides clear rules regarding the powers and responsibilities of Congress and the judiciary, the powers of the executive branch are not as clearly delineated. Historians believe that many of the framers intended for the president to be subservient to Congress except in special circumstances. Over time, the American political system has become increasingly generalized such that

Americans focus on presidential elections and give far less attention to legislative or local elections. As a result, presidents have assumed more power and have utilized executive orders and other means to dominate congressional developments. This evolutionary pattern may be one reason that Americans have grown dissatisfied with their government. Whereas Congress is composed of individuals representing a number of political views, the president and the executive branch represent one party. Presidents, especially in the modern era, have often demonstrated little effort to respond to the views of Americans representing alternative ideologies. By concentrating power behind the presidency, people can potentially see themselves as unrepresented by their government.[5] The American democratic system is organized to provide representation to the greatest number of Americans possible. However, achieving this in practice has been an elusive goal. There are many examples from American history in which a minority group achieved sufficient power and influence to force its view of American democracy on the broader population. Recent debates about abortion and immigration, for example, reflect this disproportionate influence.

The concentration of power behind the presidency is but one of the possible causes of the perceived crisis in American government. German American political scientist Yascha Mounk argued that what Americans see as democratic participation amounts to a "miniscule, near-zero, statistically non-significant impact on public policy." According to Mounk and similar theorists, the "game" of American democracy has been rigged in favor of certain individuals, who have manipulated voting systems, controlled the flow of information, and used misinformation and propaganda to marshal power to the disadvantage of most Americans and in violation of the constitutional principles of American democracy.[6] If this perception is correct, then America is a democracy in name only, and might better be described as an economic aristocracy.

On the other hand, Professor Joshua A. Geltzer of Georgetown University's Constitutional Advocacy and Protection institute argues that the proliferation of technology has led to "hyper-democratization," which he describes as a "shift away from the mediate, checked republic that America's founders carefully crafted toward an impulsive, unleashed direct democracy that's indulging the worst impulses of our most extreme elements." Geltzer summarizes, "We're increasingly ruled by an online mob. And it's a mob getting besieged with misinformation."[7] Such misinformation influences the voting and political activities of a core group but marginalizes the majority of Americans. Again, this is an example of minority rule, but one in which the views of the minority have been shaped by manipulation rather than information. Even members of this minority who trust that the government will represent their interests may have been misled into supporting political initiatives that will ultimately prove a disadvantage to them.

Some might object to the above arguments or even to the idea that American democracy is in any way in a state of crisis. But the growing concern about the state of American democracy from many directions—liberal and conservative, domestic and international—cannot be dismissed. Poll after poll has demonstrated an increasing perception that democracy is in decline and that the government does not legitimately represent the interests of the people. If a majority of Americans perceive a crisis, then by definition there is a crisis, as the health of a democracy only exists in the minds of its citizens. However, the question of why American democracy is ailing is very much in debate. Are the problems with American democracy inherent to the American democratic system itself, or a representation of how the system has been misused and abused by politicians and interest groups? Are the problems with American democracy modern or are they problems that have always plagued the American system? These are some of the questions that citizens and political analysts are struggling to answer in the hopes that determining the cause of the increasing schism between the American people and their government might lead to changes that can strengthen the American system for future generations.

Works Used

Geltzer, Joshua. "America's Problem Isn't Too Little Democracy: It's Too Much." *Politico Magazine*. June 26, 2018. Retrieved from https://www.politico.com/magazine/story/2018/06/26/america-democracy-trump-russia-2016-218894.

Longley, Robert. "Learn about Direct Democracy and Its Pros and Cons." *Thought Co.* Jan 21, 2019. Retrieved from https://www.thoughtco.com/what-is-direct-democracy-3322038.

Lucci, Micol. "This Is How Switzerland's Direct Democracy Works." *We Forum*. We Forum. Jul 31 2017. Retrieved from https://www.weforum.org/agenda/2017/07/switzerland-direct-democracy-explained/.

Mounk, Yascha. "America Is Not a Democracy." *The Atlantic*. March 2018. Retrieved from https://www.theatlantic.com/magazine/archive/2018/03/america-is-not-a-democracy/550931/.

Volokh, Eugene. "The United States Is Both a 'Republic' and a 'Democracy'—Because 'Democracy' Is Like 'Cash'." *The Washington Post*. Nov 14, 2016. Retrieved from https://www.washingtonpost.com/news/volokh-conspiracy/wp/2016/11/14/the-united-states-is-both-a-republic-and-a-democracy-because-democracy-is-like-cash/?noredirect=on&utm_term=.5be8dad54035.

Williams, Armstrong. "America's Unique Democracy." *Townhall*. Jul 12, 2011. Retrieved from https://townhall.com/columnists/armstrongwilliams/2011/07/12/americas-unique-democracy-n1376836.

Wood, Gordon S. "The Origins of American Democracy, or How the People Became Judges in Their Own Causes, the Sixty-Ninth Cleveland-Marshall Fund Lecture." *Cleveland State Law Review*. 1999. Retrieved from https://engagedscholarship.csuohio.edu/cgi/viewcontent.cgi?referer=https://www.google.com/&httpsredir=1&article=1487&context=clevstlrev.

Notes

1. Wood, "The Origins of American Democracy, or How the People Became Judges in Their Own Causes, the Sixty-Ninth Cleveland-Marshall Fund Lecture."

2. Longley, "Learn about Direct Democracy and Its Pros and Cons."
3. Lucci, "This Is How Switzerland's Direct Democracy Works."
4. Volokh, "The United States Is Both a 'Republic' and a 'Democracy'—Because 'Democracy' Is Like 'Cash'."
5. Williams, "America's Unique Democracy."
6. Mounk, "America Is Not a Democracy."
7. Geltzer, "America's Problem Isn't Too Little Democracy: It's Too Much."

20 Common Forms of Government—Study Starters

By David A. Tomar
The Quad, February 25, 2019

It's easy to criticize "the government" in broad and indirect terms, but it's far more rewarding to criticize the government using the proper terminology. And we're also guessing that these terms will be a huge help as you prepare for your civics exam, write your last philosophy essay, or navigate a last-minute political science project.

As you proceed, you'll find terms commonly used to describe forms of government. Some refer to economic policy, others to political structures, and others to philosophical ideologies. Some concepts overlap while others have no immediate parallel. It can be complex stuff.

One thing these terms have in common is each refers to an approach to governance and points to the complex, evolving, and often conflicting ideas for how we should live with one another and within a larger society.

Read on for 20 of the most commonly noted forms of governance and a few real-world examples.

1. Anarchy

Anarchism refers to the absence of government, a condition in which a nation or state operates without a central governing body. This denotes an absence of public utilities or services, a lack of regulatory control, limited diplomatic relations with other nation-states, and in most instances, a society divided into different, locally-ruled settlements (or fiefdoms).

Real World Example

Following the outbreak of civil war in 1991, and the toppling of dictator Said Barre, Somalia entered into a state of anarchy. The nation splintered into various autonomous regions, with tribal warlords claiming authority over territorial domains. Following years of involvement from the international community, the early 2000s saw the reestablishment of a transitional government, and in 2012, the passage of a constitution, which established Somalia as a "federation," or a union of partially self-governing states.

2. Aristocracy

Aristocracy refers to a form of government in which wealthy nobles are given power over those in lower socioeconomic strata. Positions of leadership are reserved for those of an elite ruling class, a status which is typically hereditary. The privileged ruling class is viewed, in this system, as possessing the education, upbringing, and genetic traits required for rulership. Aristocracy promotes an inherent class system that connects wealth and ethnicity with both the ability and right to rule.

Real World Example

Ancient Greece gives us both the word aristocracy (*aristos* = excellent; *krato* = power) as well as the concept itself. In ancient Greece, a council of empowered leading citizens were viewed as offsetting the absolute power bestowed upon a monarchy. Plato viewed the concept positively, referring to the aristocracy as being comprised of "philosopher kings," those with the knowledge and intellectual curiosity to rule as well as the requisite wealth and bloodline. But as the idea of aristocracy has become more distant from Ancient Greece, the dimensions of education and qualification have been stripped from its meaning. Today, it more largely refers to an inherently unequal form of government in which a small class of wealthy elites rules the majority population.

3. Bureaucracy

Bureaucracy refers to a form of government in which non-elected government officials carry out public responsibilities as dictated by administrative policy-making groups. In a bureaucracy, rules, regulations, procedures, and outcomes are formulated to maintain order, achieve efficiency, and prevent favoritism within the system. Bureaucracies rarely serve as forms of government on their own but are instead often used as mechanisms to underlie and strengthen overarching forms of government. Indeed, bureaucratic streamlining of policy implementation can take place under the rule of a dictator or a democracy.

Real World Example

Bureaucracy played an essential role in formalizing and equalizing taxation in Great Britain. In the 18th century, as the United Kingdom engaged in an array of military campaigns around the world, it established an encompassing taxation administration designed to the fund the war efforts. With a focus on using improved technology and more efficient collection methodologies, the United Kingdom established what would become the largest public administration network in the world to that date. The tax collection bureaucracy—the Department of Excise—served the interests of the British monarchy but would eventually give rise to the modern English bureaucracy, Her Majesty's Civil Service.

4. Capitalism

Capitalism refers to a form of economy in which production is driven by private ownership. Capitalism promotes the idea of open competition and extends from the belief that a free market economy—one with limited regulatory control—is the most efficient form of economic organization. Its advocates argue that capitalism promotes economic growth, improved standards of living, higher productivity, and broader prosperity, whereas critics argue that capitalism inherently promotes inequality, exploitation of the labor class, and unsustainable use of resources and land.

Real World Example

Capitalism takes various forms, from state and corporate capitalism to pure laissez-faire economy. Present-day United States may be referred to as a liberal market economy, in which firms engage in open competition within the con-

> **Democracy is typified by fair and free elections, civic participation, protection of human rights, and the rule of law.**

text of existing hierarchies and market mechanisms. These hierarchies and mechanisms tend to promote greater opportunities, access, and wealth for those who already enjoy an ownership stake in the U.S. economy. It also limits opportunities for mobility and shapes participation among those who do not have an ownership stake. Political influence is also directly correlated to this ownership stake within the context of American capitalism.

5. Colonialism

Colonialism is a form of governance in which a nation will seek to extend its sovereignty over other territories. In practical terms, colonialism involves the expansion of a nation's rule beyond its borders. This often entails occupation of indigenous populations and exploitation of resources to the benefit of the ruling nation. The colonizer will also often impose its own economy, culture, religious order, and form of government on an occupied people to strengthen its own authority.

Real World Example

In the 15th century, the European monarchies launched an age of nautical exploration. As merchants and conquerors voyaged in search of new lands, they found indigenous cultures whose technology and way of life they viewed as primitive. As was the tendency of European monarchies, British, French, Spanish and Dutch colonists spread their influence and authority throughout the New World, dismantling and sometimes eradicating entire cultures and peoples in the process. The most familiar case is the race for occupation of North America, the establishment of the original 13 Colonies, the systematic destruction of Native American culture, and the slave trade that gave way to the eventual independence, prosperity, and cultural identity of the United States.

6. Communism

In its purest form, Communism refers to the idea of common, public ownership of the economy, including infrastructure, utilities, and means of production. Communism, as idealized by thinkers Karl Marx and Friedrich Engels, denotes an absence of class divisions, which inherently requires the subversion of the ruling class by the working class. As such, communism often incorporates the idea of revolutionary action against unequal rule. Communism often positions itself as a counterpoint to the economic stratification underlying capitalism. This resistance to stratification sometimes also takes the form of a single-state authority, one in which political opposition or dissidence may be restricted. This may manifest in some communist states as a more authoritarian form of governance, as typified by the Soviet brand of communism that swept the globe during the mid-20th century.

Real World Example

Modern communism manifests as a descendant from Soviet communism—both ideologically and materially—and is sometimes identified as the Marxist-Leninist variation on communism. Countries that retain a single-party, Marxist-Leninist rulership include Cuba, Laos, Vietnam, and the People's Republic of China. Each of these nations adopted this form of government at the height of the Cold War—between the 1940s and 1960s—under the auspices of Russian influence. While the Soviet communist government crumbled in 1991, these nations remain committed to their own version of the Marxist-Leninist ideology. Though North Korea refers to itself as communist, the singularity of its rulership hews much closer to dictatorship.

7. Democracy

Democracy refers to a form of government in which the people are given a direct role in choosing their leadership. Its primary goal is governance through fair representation, a system in which no single force or entity can exercise unchecked control or authority. The result is a system which requires discourse, debate, and compromise to satisfy the broadest possible number of public interests. Democracy is typified by fair and free elections, civic participation, protection of human rights, and the rule of law.

Real World Example

While the notion of democracy finds its roots in Greek antiquity, its practice became the particular province of settlers in the colonies of the United States. In the years leading up to the U.S. War for Independence, the philosophical impetus of governance through representation played an important role in building the case for revolt. It was also essential, as the framers of the Constitution constructed a way of life around a concept called "representative democracy." The colonists imported the racial, ethnic, and socioeconomic inequalities of their European predecessors. But in representative democracy and the Constitution, they also forged a framework for the marginalized to fight for their representation. Today, just over half of the world's nations self-identify as constitutional democracies.

8. Federalism

Federalism is a form of government that both combines and divides powers between a centralized federal authority and an array of regional and local authorities. This is typically a system in which a set of states, territories, or provinces are both self-governing and beholden to the authority of a broad, unifying government structure. This is considered a balance in approach that provides roughly equal status of authority to two distinct levels of government.

Real World Example

The United States was among the first true examples of a federation, a nation comprised from set regions, each with its own unique set of customs, laws, and demographic compositions. Today, much philosophical debate exists over what level of independent authority states have versus the level of central control that the federal government has over state laws. This debate—and the never-ending stream of constitutional and judicial questions that arise from it—keep the state and federal authority in constant and dynamic flux.

9. Feudalism

Feudalism is a social structure revolving around land ownership, nobility, and military obligation. Though not a formal way of governing, feudalism refers to a way of life in which sharp, hierarchical divisions separate noble classes, clergy, and peasantry. Opportunities for movement between these hierarchies is largely impossible. In this system, peasants typically provided labor and military service in exchange for occupancy of land and protection from outside forces under the authority of a noble lord. In turn, lordships, or fiefdoms, often engaged one another politically, economically, and militarily. Feudalism was a highly decentralized and agrarian way of life supplanted when the European monarchies created the infrastructure to impose central rule over their various dominions.

Real World Example

France of the 11th century is particularly noteworthy for the decentralization of power and the splintering of rulership into many smaller entities. During this period, travel through France would take one through a series of fiefdoms in which small, ruling families would charge various fees for passage, participation in trade, or use of the woodlands. Though feudalism would become largely extinct with the rise of the monarchy, this brief revolution in France would represent a moment of evolution for the ideas of private ownership and personal power.

10. Kleptocracy

Kleptocracy is a form of government in which the ruling party has either come to power, retained power, or both, through means of corruption and theft. This is not a form of government that a ruling class would ever self-apply but a pejorative term used to describe a group whose power rests on a foundation of embezzlement, misappropriation of funds, and the transfer of massive amounts of wealth from public to private interests. These private interests will typically overlap the ruling party's own economic interests.

Real World Example

Vladamir Putin's post-Soviet Russia is a clear example of kleptocratic behavior by a ruling class. In the early 1990s, as the former Soviet Union collapsed and confusion reigned, Putin and his allies from within the leadership of the KGB squirreled away billions of dollars in public money. They would ultimately use this money to fund a rise to power and, subsequently, the establishment of a quasi-authoritative regime that handed central banking authority over to cronies, awarded friends with enormous no-bid contracts to build the notoriously shoddy Sochi Olympic Village, and, in 2003, took control of a privately owned oil company. In the latter case, Putin demonstrated his absolute power by claiming fraud against oil magnate Mikhail Khodorkovsky. The charges led to the billionaire's imprisonment for a decade and parceling of his Yukos Oil Company to Putin's friends and allies. In spite of its democratic facade, Putin's Russia meets the basic qualifications of a true kleptocracy.

11. Meritocracy

Meritocracy refers to a system in which authority is vested in those who have demonstrated the merits deemed pertinent to governing or public administration. Often, these merits are conferred through testing and academic credentials and are meant to create an order in which talents, abilities, and intellect determine who should hold positions of leadership and economic stewardship. The result is a social hierarchy based on achievement.

Real World Example

In a sense, America's educational tradition suggests a meritocracy in which higher degrees denote access to greater opportunity. However, because earning this degree does not itself confer any automatic authority upon a person, the U.S. is not a true meritocracy. Today, Singapore offers a modern example that aligns closest to the concept of meritocracy. Here, academic achievements play a deeply determinant role in opportunities for economic advancement, professional mobility, and civic leadership. Though this approach has helped Singapore to become a thriving economy, some express concern that its meritocracy enforces sharp hierarchical divisions between members of the public and a small population of intellectual elites.

12. Military Dictatorship

A dictatorship is a nation ruled with absolute power, in the absence of a democratic process, and typically under the thumb of a single authority figure. In a military dictatorship, this authority usually heads the nation's armed forces. A military dictatorship often comes to power by subverting the existing seat of government—sometimes though claims of corruption, weakness, or ineffectiveness—and which subsequently uses the military to establish its own brand of law and order. Military dictatorships will frequently prioritize law and order over due process, civil liberties, or political freedoms. Dissent or political opposition can be dangerous or even deadly for those living under a military dictatorship.

Real World Example

In 2014, Thailand's general election was disrupted by widespread protests against the government. The result was a nullified election and the subsequent dismantling of the civilian government. In the vacuum of power, General Prayut Chan-o-cha declared martial law, dissolved the senate, and placed himself in control of the nation. Since then, Thailand has persisted under dictatorial military rule. The military junta, called the National Council for Peace and Order, imposed nationwide curfews, forbids political gatherings, threatens arrest for political opponents or activists, controls the media, and enforces widespread internet censorship.

13. Monarchy

Monarchy refers to a form of rule in which absolute power and authority are held by a single member of a royal bloodline. In a monarchy, the individual in the seat of power is often believed to have been placed there by "divine right," or the will of God. In a monarchical society, power is inherited within a line of succession that relates to one's bloodline and birth-order within the ruling royal family. Though the monarchy has historically indicated absolute power, the concept has become increasingly diluted with the evolution of democratic principles. Today, some monarchies exist but are merely symbolic, whereas others coexist within constitutional structures. However, until the 19th century, monarchy was the most common form of government in the world.

Real World Example

Today, 45 nations in the world are governed by some form of monarchy. In many cases, this monarchy is largely symbolic and subservient to a constitution, as with the 16 commonwealth states recognizing Britain's Queen Elizabeth II. By contrast, monarchies continue to enjoy far-reaching political authority in Brunei, Liechtenstein, Monaco, Morocco, Oman, Qatar, Saudi Arabia, and Swaziland.

14. Oligarchy

Oligarchy refers to a form of government in which a smattering of individuals rule over a nation. In many ways, oligarchy is a catch-all for any number of other forms of governance in which a specific set of qualities—wealth, heredity, race—are used to vest power in a small group of individuals. So, forms of government regarded as aristocratic, plutocratic, or totalitarian, for instance, can be referred to as oligarchic.

Oligarchies are often characterized by tyrannical or authoritarian rule and an absence of democratic practices or individual rights.

Real World Example

The apartheid government that ruled South Africa from 1948 to 1991 was a racially constructed oligarchy, one in which the minority white population exercised dominance and imposed segregation over the nation's black population. The minority population controlled policy, public administration, and law enforcement, all to the explicit end of oppressing South Africa's majority black population. The concentration of power in the hands of a minority population as a function of racial identity, as well as the resultant authoritarian rule vested in this minority population, qualifies South Africa's now defunct apartheid government as an oligarch. Today, even with the Apartheid government dismantled, the vestiges of racial inequality remain in South Africa's economy and political structures.

15. Plutocracy

Plutocracy refers to a system of rule in which power is determined as a direct function of wealth. Plutocracy mirrors the economic hierarchy of aristocratic systems but lacks the philosophical imperatives used to justify the latter. Whereas aristocratic forms of governance justified economic hierarchy by presuming an equivalence between wealth, heredity, and the qualification to lead, plutocracy refers in simpler terms to the ascendance of the wealthy to positions of power. Think of it as the difference between "old money" and "new money." As with the phrase "new money" itself, plutocracy is rarely a term that a ruling class will self-apply. Rather, it is often used as a derogatory term meant to highlight the inequality inherent in capitalist societies.

Real World Example

The label of plutocracy has been lobbed against a number of societies over the course of history and generally as a way of critiquing inequality. In both the United States and post-Soviet Russia—where a select group of billionaires possess 50% and 35%, respectively, of all national wealth—social critics have identified patterns of plutocracy. These critics would argue that the outsize power and influence of the wealthy in these societies tends to undermine equality and fair economic competition.

16. Republicanism

Republicanism, the form of government—not to be conflated with the Republican political party specific to U.S. politic—refers to a system in which power is vested in the citizenry. In technical definition, a republic is a nation in which the people hold popular sovereignty through the electoral and legislative processes as well as through participation in public and civic life. In its earliest form, the republic was perceived as a counterbalance to monarchy, an approach which merged monarchy and aristocracy with some trappings of democracy.

Real World Example

Informed by the philosophical ideals of the enlightenment, particularly the writing of Jean-Jacques Rousseau, the revolutionaries who toppled the French monarchy in the 1790s established a new republic in their wake. Though the République française was short-lived—Napoleon's rule transformed France into an aristocracy by the turn of the next century—its founding on the principles of Rousseau's Social Contract would be particularly influential to the myriad nations soon to emerge from crumbling European monarchies and splintering colonial empires.

17. Socialism

Socialism refers to a form of government in which the people own the primary means of production. A counterpoint to the competitive nature and unequal proclivities of capitalism, socialism has existed in many forms and to widely variant degrees of strictness throughout history and around the world. From small communal societies to state-level governments that provide encompassing public services such as universal healthcare, the concept of socialism permeates governments the world over. By contrast to the less compromising and often more authoritarian nature of communism, socialism tends to be a malleable concept. Some adherents view socialism as referring to a strict policy of shared ownership and equal distribution of resources, while others believe free market capitalism can coexist with socialist forms of public administration. To wit, the Social Security system of the declaratively capitalist United States is inherently socialist in nature.

Real World Example

The Nordic model of social democracy represents perhaps the most effective real world implementation of socialist principles. The Scandinavian nations of Denmark, Finland, Iceland, Norway, and Sweden adhere to policies that combine free market capitalism with extensive public works, including free healthcare, free education, a comprehensive welfare state, and high percentages of unionized workers. This approach essentially combines the social consciousness of socialism with the private ownership and competitive opportunity of capitalism.

18. Theocracy

Theocracy refers to a form of government in which a specific religious ideology informs the leadership, laws, and customs of a nation. In many instances, there will be little to no distinction between scriptural laws and legal codes. Likewise, religious clergy will typically occupy roles of leadership, and in some instances, the highest office in the nation. Because religious law usually extends from writings and traditions that are many centuries old, and therefore impose practices that may not conform with present-day standards of ethical justice or constitutional law, theocracies frequently run afoul of organizations and agencies advocating for global human rights.

Real World Example

Iran is perhaps the most important and powerful theocratic state in the world today. Since a 1979 Islamic student revolution toppled the Iranian monarchy, the ayatollahs have ruled the country. Here, a "supreme leader" serves as head of state and delegates authority to other religious leaders. In Iran, the elected president is subservient to this supreme Islamic scholar. Likewise, while Iran has developed some dimensions of a modern legal code, judiciary system, and administrative process, all of these must first be based on Islamic criteria. In essence, the Sharia—the primary legal doctrine of the Islamic faith—is the primary legal doctrine for the nation of Iran.

19. Totalitarianism

Totalitarianism is an authoritarian form of government in which the ruling party recognizes no limitations whatsoever on its power, either in the public life or private rights of its citizens. Power is often vested in the hands of a single figure, an authority around whom significant propaganda is built as a way of extending and retaining uncontested authority. Totalitarian states often employ widespread surveillance, control over mass media, intimidating demonstrations of paramilitary or police power, and suppression—usually violent—of protest, activism, or political opposition.

Real World Example

Though North Korea identifies itself as the Democratic People's Republic of Korea, this is truly the clearest example of a totalitarian dictatorship in the modern world. Kim Jong-un rules with singular and unchallenged authority, commanding over his public without political opposition. With absolute control over the state-run media, an enormous military apparatus at his disposal, and an endless cycle of propaganda and misinformation helping to sustain his power, Kim Jong-un rules his state in a vacuum from world affairs. Criticism of the supreme leader or protest of his policies is a crime punishable by death, as are countless other crimes for which due process is not required. North Korea's propensity toward human rights violations is said to be unparalleled in the modern world.

20. Tribalism

Tribalism refers to a form of governance in which there is an absence of central authority and where, instead, various regional tribes lay claim to different territories, resources, or domains. In this system, trade, commerce, and war may occur between different tribes without the involvement or oversight of a unifying structure. This was a particularly common way of life in the premodern world, where different families and clans would establish a set of common rules and rituals specific to their community. While many tribes have forms of internal leadership—from councils and chiefdoms to warlords and patriarchs—tribes are also distinct for having relatively limited role differentiation or role stratification within. In some regards, this can make the customs internal to some tribes particularly egalitarian. That said, tribalism as a way of life has been threatened, and in many parts of the world extinguished, by modernity, development, and the imposition of outside authority.

Real World Example

Afghanistan is a nation naturally predisposed to tribalism. Centuries of interference from outside invaders—the Soviet Union and the United States chief among them—have created an ongoing state of disarray for the central government of Afghanistan. This—combined with a sprawling and treacherous geography—reduced Afghanistan to a state of regional tribes. In many instance, the authority of local warlords, drug cartels, or Islamic clergy take on far more immediate importance than the authority of a central government. Today, the tribal dynamics that permeate Afghanistan represent a more direct influence on the lives of local populations than any international or federal ruling structure.

Of course, this is just a quick overview of a vast subject. Each of these forms of government carries an array of complex philosophical, ethical, and practical questions. May this summary serve as a starting point as you plunge into your research.

The deeper dive is up to you!

Print Citations

CMS: Tomar, David A. "20 Common Forms of Government—Study Starters." In *The Reference Shelf: Democracy Evolving,* edited by Micah L. Issitt, 9-19. Amenia, NY: Grey House Publishing, 2019.

MLA: Tomar, David A. "20 Common Forms of Government—Study Starters." *The Reference Shelf: Democracy Evolving,* edited by Micah L. Issitt, Grey Housing Publishing, 2019, pp. 9-19.

APA: Tomar, D.A. (2019). 20 commons forms of government—Study starters. In Micah L. Issitt (Ed.), *The reference shelf: Democracy evolving* (pp. 9-19). Amenia, NY: Grey Housing Publishing.

What Exactly Is Neoliberalism?

By Kean Birch
The Conversation, **November 2, 2017**

I struggle with neoliberalism—as a problematic economic system we might want to change—and as an analytical term people increasingly use to describe that system.

I've been reading and writing about the concept for more than a decade. But the more I read, the more I think that neoliberalism is losing its analytical edge.

As a result of its growing popularity in academia, media and popular discussions, it's crucial to understand neoliberalism as a concept. We need to know its origins and its definition in order to understand our current political and economic mess, including the rise of nativism that played a part in Brexit and Donald Trump's election a year ago.

Neoliberalism is regularly used in popular debate around the world to define the last 40 years. It's used to refer to an economic system in which the "free" market is extended to every part of our public and personal worlds. The transformation of the state from a provider of public welfare to a promoter of markets and competition helps to enable this shift.

Neoliberalism is generally associated with policies like cutting trade tariffs and barriers. Its influence has liberalized the international movement of capital, and limited the power of trade unions. It's broken up state-owned enterprises, sold off public assets and generally opened up our lives to dominance by market thinking.

As a term, neoliberalism is increasingly used across popular media, including *The New York Times*, *The Times* (of London) and *The Daily Mail*. It's also used within international institutions like the World Economic Forum, the Organisation for Economic Co-operation and Development and the International Monetary Fund.

Neoliberalism a Trump Antidote?

Neoliberalism is criticized for giving markets too much power over our lives. Yet in light of the rise of Donald Trump and other nativist, anti-trade populists, there is a growing chorus of people extolling the virtues of neoliberalism.

What's most evident from this growing popular debate about neoliberalism—whether from left-leaning critics or right-leaning advocates—is that there are many different views of neoliberalism; not just what it means politically, but just as critically, what it means analytically.

This raises an important question: How do we use a term like "neoliberalism" when so many people have such different understandings of what it means?

I wrestled with this question when writing my book, *A Research Agenda for Neoliberalism*, in which I examine the intellectual history of neoliberalism. I do so in order to examine the different conceptions of the term and to expose the contradictions underlying our daily use of it.

The term "neoliberalism" has a fascinating intellectual history. It appears as long ago as 1884 in an article by R.A. Armstrong for *The Modern Review* in which he defined liberals who promoted state intervention in the economy as "neo-liberal"—almost the exact opposite meaning from its popular and academic use today.

Another early appearance is in an 1898 article for *The Economic Journal* by Charles Gide in which he used the term to refer to an Italian economist, Maffeo Pantaleoni, who argued that we need to promote a "hedonistic world . . . in which free competition will reign absolutely"—somewhat closer to our current conception.

Adopted by Liberal Thinkers

As the 20th century dawned and the world moved through one World War and onto the next, the term was appropriated by a range of liberal thinkers who felt sidelined by the ascendance of state planning and socialism.

The conventional narrative is that "neo-liberalism" was first proposed as a term to describe a rebooted liberalism in the 1930s after the so-called Walter Lippman Colloquium held in Paris in 1938.

However, its history is not as clear cut as this narrative might imply. According to Arnaud Brennetot, for example, the term was subsequently mainly used to refer to French and other liberals associated with a publishing house called La Libraire de Medicis at least until the early 1950s. By then, the term was increasingly used to refer to German Ordoliberalism, which was a "neoliberal" school based on the idea that markets need a strong state in order to protect competition—ideas that are a major forerunner of the European Union's framework conditions.

> **How do we use a term like "neoliberalism" when so many people have such different understandings of what it means?**

Famously, Milton Friedman even referred to himself as a "neoliberal" in a 1951 article for the Norwegian magazine *Farmand*, although he subsequently dropped the term.

By the 1970s, Brennetot and others argued that neoliberalism was a term primarily associated with a shifting emphasis in Latin America away from import-substitution policies towards open economies, influenced by Chicago School thinkers like Friedman.

It was around this time that neoliberalism increasingly took on negative overtones, especially after the violent overthrow of Salvador Allende's government in Chile in 1973. As the 1980s dawned, along with the generally accepted birth of the modern neoliberal era, the term "neoliberalism" became indelibly linked to the Chicago School of Economics (as well as Law and Business).

Neoliberalism Has Several 'Schools'

When we use the term today, it's generally with this Chicago inflection, rather than its other previous and alternative histories and associations.

But it's important to remember that there were and are at least seven schools of neoliberalism. Some of the older schools, like the First Chicago School (of Frank Knight, Henry Simons, Jacob Viner), disappeared or were subsumed in later schools—in this case, the Second Chicago School (of Milton Friedman, Aaron Director, George Stigler).

Other old schools, like the Italian or Bocconi School (of Maffeo Pantaleoni, Luigi Einaudi) faded into academia before being resurrected as the legitimization for current austerity policies. Other more marginal schools, like the Virginia School (of James Buchanan, Gordon Tullock)—itself influenced by the Italian school—have existed under the radar until recent critiques by historians like Nancy MacLean.

As these various schools of neoliberal thought have evolved and mutated over time, so too have our understandings of them and their influence on us. It's therefore tricky to identify neoliberalism with any one particular school of thought without missing out on a whole lot of the story.

Three Contradictions

That's a major reason why I identify three core contradictions in our current understandings of neoliberalism in my new book.

First, too little has been done analytically to address the contradiction between the supposed extension of "free" markets under neoliberalism and the growth in market power and dominance of corporate entities and monopolies like Google and Microsoft.

Second, there has been too much emphasis on the idea that our lives, identities and subjectivities under neoliberalism are framed by "entrepreneurial" beliefs, attitudes and thinking.

In contrast, my view is that our lives, societies, and economies are dominated by diverse forms of rentiership—for example home ownership, intellectual property monopolies and market control. According to British academic Guy Standing, rentiership can be defined as the extraction of income from the "ownership, possession or control of assets that are scarce or artificially made scarce."

Finally, there has been little interest in trying to understand the important role of contract and contract law—as opposed to "markets"—in the organization of neoliberal capitalism.

All these areas need addressing in order to better understand our future, but neoliberalism has perhaps run its course in providing us with the necessary analytical tools to do this work. It's time to find new ways to think about our world.

Print Citations

CMS: Birch, Kean. "What Exactly Is Neoliberalism?" In *The Reference Shelf: Democracy Evolving,* edited by Micah L. Issitt, 20-23. Amenia, NY: Grey House Publishing, 2019.

MLA: Birch, Kean. "What Exactly Is Neoliberalism?" *The Reference Shelf: Democracy Evolving,* edited by Micah L. Issitt, Grey Housing Publishing, 2019, pp. 20-23.

APA: Birch, K. (2019). What exactly is neoliberalism? In Micah L. Issitt (Ed.), *The reference shelf: Democracy evolving* (pp. 20-23). Amenia, NY: Grey Housing Publishing.

Democracy's Midlife Crisis: An Interview with David Runciman

By David Runciman, Danielle Charette, and Jacob Hamburger
Tocqueville 21, February 19, 2019

David Runciman is head of the department of politics and international studies at Cambridge University and host of the popular podcast Talking Politics. Danielle Charette and Jacob Hamburger interviewed him last week in Chicago about his most recent book, How Democracy Ends.

Originally published on Tocqueville 21, a Franco-American web magazine about contemporary democracy, this interview has been lightly edited and condensed for clarity.

Jacob Hamburger: Your presentation of the "end" of democracy rests on a distinction between three different time-scales. First, we go back to Athens; second, the American and French revolutions; and third, the rise of mass suffrage and the bureaucratic state after World War I. … I'm interested in your thoughts on how Tocqueville's idea of "equality of conditions" might "end" in the same way you think about these other stories ending.

David Runciman: The long story has, at its heart, an idea of a form of equality—of political equality—and the idea that we can control our own fate. That's the deep-buried thing. But it's a mistake to think even that is timeless. Some ideas are dead. No one now believes in the divine right of kings. Equality could end up like that too. There must be a serious possibility that we move to a form of social and political and economic and moral organization where that idea seems dead. I don't think we're there yet, but there are glimpses of it in our world. In *Homo Deus*, Yuval Harari writes that we are at the end of history, not for Francis Fukuyama's reasons, but because history is the story of human beings believing that they can control their own fate—and that's about to end, because we're about to enter the phase when we will just become data points in a vast information-processing system. Now, if he's right, and that happens in the next fifty years, then that is the end of the idea of deep democracy.

Danielle Charette: Your central theme is that our democracy is "middle-aged." Is a middle-aged democracy just utterly unable to cope with such an apocalyptic vision?

DR: Well, it's "middle-aged" only in our relatively short story. It's not middle-aged in the long story. This thing that we think of as democracy is a product of the First and Second World Wars. In stable democracies, we're seventy, or maybe one hundred years in. To say it's middle-aged is to say, like with middle-aged people, your life is not over. You can change your life. It doesn't have to be like this. There may be points when you think it's just all pointless, a long (or short) road to oblivion, but you can reinvent yourself. You can decide what's of real value.

Part of growing old as a human being and of moving into old age is that you have to make some choices. But if you make the right choices, your life could become better. So, I'm arguing against the idea that we're just on the edge of the abyss. We're in the middle of some story. The point of it is that change is really hard, particularly when you're quite comfortable—which democracies are. We sometimes think it's easier than it is because we think we're younger than we are. We think we're teenage democracies, where the upside is much bigger and the downside is much bigger, where the future is wide-open. Middle-aged people find it really hard to change. So maybe no, you can't cope. Also, speaking as a middle-aged person, I can say that we learn lots of good avoidance techniques. You become quite skilled at not facing the bad stuff.

DC: In other words, it's time for some serious psychotherapy.

DR: Yes! I say in the book, part of what's needed is therapy, because democracies are acting out. They're middle-aged and behaving as if they're much younger. Part of it is nostalgia and part of it is a midlife crisis. They're just doing these insane things! But the solution to a midlife crisis is not to buy the motorbike or have the affair—it's to get therapy.

JH: The book is primarily about Western European and American democracy, so you're not necessarily attributing these characteristics to democracies around the world.

DR: Definitely not.

JH: But then the question is, to what extent does what happens in these advanced democracies, these middle-aged democracies, spill over into democracies in other parts of the world? Brazilian democracy is about the same age as Spanish or Portuguese democracy, which we'd have the instinct to see as closer to your story. But, then when you look at what's going on in Brazil, the consequences start to resemble the crises of the "young" democracies of the 1930s.

DR: I think that's right. It's important to say that this is not just a crude number-of-years thing. It's, as it were, the time in which the various elements that make a stable democracy have come together. Spanish democracy looks pretty stable to me, and it's only, what, forty years old? But Brazilian democracy looks a lot less stable. But even during those forty years, it's been less stable. Spain had the advantage that it was quickly taken into a stable European order. With somewhere like Brazil, you could argue there hasn't been a very long period at all where democracy feels like the bedrock of politics. It feels quite contingent. It is, unquestionably much more vulnerable. In the same way, I think Turkish democracy is quite a long story, and Turks will tell you it's at least a hundred years old. But it's not continuous; it's been punctuated by coups, as in the Brazilian case. It's not stable, and bits of the package have always been really contested.

Indian democracy is relatively old in these terms, and in some respects has a middle-aged feel to it. But, in other respects, it looks much younger and more open, with both upsides and downsides. So I definitely don't think you can just find the date of the democratic constitution, calculate the years, and say—using J. Richard Gott's "Copernican principle"—we're half-way through, so Brazil will be fine for the next forty years! Brazil may not be fine for the next forty weeks. But I don't think, even in those forty years, it was ever secure for forty-week periods.

JH: One a way that people often describe the current moment is to say that we're in the age of "strongman politics." People talk about a "strongman international," between Trump, Orbán, Putin, Erdoğan, Modi, and now, Bolsonaro. And what's powerful about your metaphor of the middle-aged man buying a motorcycle is that there's something really impotent about it. Trump is the best example, because he's this guy who likes to talk tough but is in fact a very weak and ineffective leader.

DR: Absolutely. There is an axis of politics which is uncannily similar, in so many ways: the role of families (particularly daughters), the use of social media (not just Twitter, but particularly Twitter), the rhetorical tropes, the conspiracies. It's almost as if they went to conspiracy theory school together. So yes, that applies regardless whether the democracy is two hundred years old, or, in the Hungarian case, 25 years old. The politicians seem to be behaving in the same way.

But I think that kind of political behavior is very different in different situations. I wrote a piece a few months ago in the *London Review of Books*, the headline of which is "The U.S. is not Hungary." In the Hungarian case, this politics is not impotent, because the institutions are impotent, actually. The institutions were weak and shallow; they had shallow roots. I think it makes a huge difference if there is a society where no one has a memory of anything other than stable democratic politics, and a society where half the population lived half their lives with a different kind of politics and where the rule of law and a free media are, for most people, things they never even grew up with. So the strongman in Hungary has, like Putin, co-opted the institutions.

That rhetoric in the United States just bounces off some very durable and robust institutions. People say that Orbán has captured the Supreme Court, and now Trump is capturing the U.S. Supreme Court. No he's not! He's put on the Supreme Court two completely conventional, mainstream judges. He hasn't put "Trump judges." He might try, but he will fail. There's no way the Supreme Court has been captured by Trump. It's been captured by the Republican Party, but that's been a fifty-year project. That's not a strongman project at all.

Bolsonaro's rhetoric can galvanize political violence, including street violence. With Trump, there's been some violence, I know. A BBC journalist got mildly beaten up. Now, I'm not trying to downplay that. But seriously, that's not the breakdown of democracy. It's pretty unpleasant, but, in Brazil, people voted for Bolsonaro because they wanted guns. And in India, like in China, there are one hundred million young men who will not find a partner because one hundred million women are missing. Now, you throw "strongman" rhetoric into that society, and it's different from throwing that rhetoric into a society of Medicare, Medicaid, and angry Midwesterners. I think we overstate the rhetorical similarity, both between countries and across time. Take someone from the 1930s and show them our world, and yes, they will recognize the way these strongmen do politics. But the overall story is different.

DC: Maybe it's just that our horizon for hope has narrowed, but having written a book titled How Democracy Ends, *you seem, for the moment, relatively optimistic.*

DR: There's a very different take in the U.S. than in the U.K. People in the U.K. think that it's quite a depressing book. And in the U.S., my publisher read it, and she said, "This book really cheered me up." And I said, "Why?" She replied, "Because I genuinely thought Trump was the end of democracy, and you're saying it's going to survive!"

Brexit is like living through a really boring bureaucratic nightmare. Trump is like living through a soap opera. And Brexit is just soul-destroying, because it's pointless and no one knows what's going on. For people in Britain, this story, which is of more gradual decline and being stuck in middle age and wanting to change but being afraid to change, chimes to the moment. It seems to Brits: this is how democracy ends. It might take fifty years, but we're just winding this thing down. Whereas in the U.S., there's now this sense that if we can survive the next two years, it's going to be great again! We'll elect Kamala Harris, and it'll be rainbows!

DC: Perhaps one of the sources for hopefulness is how you describe the different temporal metaphors. Tocqueville begins with man in the cradle: man is born. And Arendt runs with that; there's so much focus on natality. But I know you have a longstanding interest in Hobbes, who is motivated by the reality of death. Do you see the middle-age metaphor as a compromise between death and natality?

DR: It's absolutely part of the point. I'm doing two things by saying we're middle-aged. I'm saying that societies are literally full of old people, and that the institutions are quite old and tired, too. We know more about what it is for a person to be fifty, sixty, seventy years old than about what it is for a democracy to be fifty, sixty, or seventy years old. There is some despair about growing old, but for the most part, people don't actually give up hope.

I saw a story in the paper yesterday on human contentment. There's an arc from ages fifty to seventy where measurable happiness actually increases. That cheered me up, since I'm fifty-one! The human condition is not that, once you get past a certain point, you're just waiting for death. The best years may be ahead of you. But you can't hanker for your youth. You have to believe that you are capable of change. You will be miserable if you just cling on to the thing that you have. After you park your motorbike in the garage, after you have a bit of therapy, you have to actually think: what do I want to do with the rest of my life? And it's the same with democracy. We shouldn't quit elections. But maybe we should do citizens' democracy. Maybe let's actually think local democracy is more important than national democracy. I don't know if that's optimism, but it's anti-fatalism.

JH: On that note, last night, you touched briefly on the New Green Deal. And elsewhere you've advocated another experimental idea: extending the vote to children. When we're taking about how democracy moves past its middle age, do you think a big ambitious project, like the Green New Deal, is enough in itself, inserted into the normal election cycle, to do that? A more pessimistic take that you hear a lot is, that that's a great idea, but societies will only go through real radical change when there's a depression or a war.

DR: I slightly regret that proposal for giving the vote to six-year-olds. I still believe it, but it became a news story in the U.K. My son, who's now at university, read the story in the *Guardian* and said, if he had to summarize it, the headline he would have put on it is, "Cambridge academic ties shoelaces together and falls over in public."

But what surprised me most about advocating the vote for six-year-olds was that it provoked outrage. I got torrents of messages—and I'm not on Twitter, so people have to take the trouble to email me! I wanted to ask, what's so dangerous about this? What do you think the risk is here, relative to these insane risks that we're running with a political system that clearly can't cope? If you were to

> **Today, educated people look at politicians and think 'They're just like us. What gives them the right to rule and not us?'**

lower the voting age to six, all that would happen is that politicians would have to go into schools, so they would probably end up behaving better. What's the worst that would happen? It's not as if six-year-olds would run the country. There aren't enough of them!

Somehow, we've got our risk profiles wrong. We know we need to do something big and dramatic, but we won't touch the thing that's the barrier in our way of doing something big and dramatic. People seem to think that the danger is in constitutional or electoral reform when the planet is burning. I don't get it. People say we need something like a Green New Deal—a radical new politics—but we won't touch the political system that we have, because that's too dangerous, which to me is insane.

JH: Are you saying even the Green New Deal isn't radical enough, because it doesn't touch the way politics is organized?

DR: Well it is radical. It wants to radically change what the state does. It's pretty ambitious, but without fundamentally being brave about the democracy that we have. I think in the U.S., it's very hard, isn't it, to sound like you're not fully signed up. Even if you're Alexandria Ocasio-Cortez, you have to still believe in the founding myths, don't you?

DC: It's probably easier to go after the myths that the electoral structure.

DR: Right. I'm not saying it's just a question of reforming the electoral structure and then the Green New Deal would flow through. It's more that, in middle age, there are things you think you can and can't change. And where middle-aged people go wrong is they change the wrong things. They don't address the thing at the root. They have the affair, they buy the motorbike. They don't address what's making them unhappy.

JH: Is it also that you have to fit your ideas for a radical future into these familiar past categories, like the New Deal?

DR: Yes, it's really striking to me. We're so obsessed with the 1930s. It's either fascism, or the New Deal. To which I would say: it's definitely neither fascism, nor the New Deal. There are these motifs, and the New Deal is one of them. People have been looking for the "New" New Deal for a long time. This is not the 1930s. The social, and the economic, and, frankly, the cultural conditions are not the same.

JH: Is there something about our moment in history that makes us look for these easy comparisons? Or is that just how people do politics, giving voters something they can recognize?

DR: We're in a phase where we're going to see quite a lot of new politics and coalition-building. It's happening a lot around Europe: some really surprising, new—not always particularly attractive—coalitions being built across various social, educational, generational divides. There's a big prize in particular for the politician who can bridge either the educational or the generational divide

That's another thing about being middle-aged, which is you have more past experience to draw upon. If you're eighteen, you don't spend your time thinking, which bit of my life does this remind me of? You think that you've just become an adult, and the future is open. If you are America, you have too much baggage, because you've got a life that you've lived, and it's really hard. And if you're Hungary, there isn't a democratic story, so Orbán tells the thousand years of Christendom. The hard thing is recognizing that the future is still open.

JH: When you look at the Gilets Jaunes *movement, do you see this sort of deep questioning going on?*

DR: You do, and it touches on a really striking feature of democratic politics around the world: the educational question. Traditionally, in representative democracy, elected representatives were a class apart. Today, educated people look at politicians and think: They're just like us. What gives them the right to rule and not us?

Everyone else looks at politicians and thinks: Not only are they nothing like us, but they're like all those other people. What gives that whole group the right?

DC: So neither the trustee nor the delegate model of representation, but the disgruntled neighbor model?

DR: Yes, that anger is real. There have got to be ways to channel this better than the Yellow Vests movement. But it is striking that it's got such legs. And its supporters are saying, we're going to bring down Macron. This man—who won by 66 percent—he's not legitimate in their eyes. That is radical. It's not the violence. The violence is radical too, but it's familiar. What is quite unusual, in the history of the successful period of modern democracy, is to reject representation.

JH: I get the sense you're excited about some of these calls for infusing democracy with new kinds of participation structures, but at the same time, I hear some deep skepticism about the ability to actively take the referendums that the Yellow Vests want to integrate into the French system and actually fuse those with what we've got now.

DR: I think we should be excited and open, particularly in systems that have been remarkably unchanging. We forget how weird it is that some of the basic arrangements of our democracy have remained unchanged over decades, and in some cases hundreds of years. We should be excited by the thought that we're starting, finally, to change some of that. But it's really hard. And part of what makes it hard is that people always say, but we don't want to actually change it. We just want to add things on that make it work better. That's the basic thought: We'll introduce citizens' assemblies or forms of deliberation, or forms of participation, or maybe even replace the House of Lords with a randomly selected group in order to enhance the basic function of the representative assembly. It'll make it work better.

Well, first of all, it probably won't work better. They'll be in tension with one another. And second of all, why is the project a rescue project? Why isn't it a radical rethinking? And you do see examples—Brexit being the classic—where people think, we've got this system, it's a bit tired, it doesn't really work, so we'll give it a little injection of popular participation and then we'll let the system live with the consequences. The society isn't going to fall apart, but politics is just going to grind to a halt. British politics is just in quick sand.

DC: Finally, I know you're fascinated by Silicon Valley culture, where at the fringes, there are people who want to abolish death. If someone came to you with that proposal, is that an example of radical new thinking? Or is that a refusal of reality and of democracy?

DR: It fits with the middle-aged metaphor. The other way you can go with this is to try to jump straight to immortality. I think it's dangerous, and also weird. And there's something abhorrent about the sense of privilege of someone who would use his tens of billions to try to buy himself eternal life. I don't want Peter Thiel-style radicalism: "just smash it up and see what happens." That seems what it's always been:

pretty irresponsible. I believe in political responsibility. I believe politics is thinking about the unintended consequences of what you do. I believe people should be answerable for their actions. And abolishing death seems to cut against that.

JH: Is this related to why you think Mark Zuckerberg is a bigger threat than Donald Trump? Both are irresponsible, but Zuckerberg might have more power to do what he actually wants to do with democracy than Trump does?

DR: The thing with Trump is, what you see is what you get. We understand the accountability framing around him. He understands it too. He sees the barriers, just as we do. And they might break, but, in a way, we know what it would be to hold him down. With Zuckerberg, it's much harder to see, and some of the conventional restraints within his own corporation are unconstrained. And it's not like the shareholders are holding him to account.

I'm more frightened by people who don't understand their power than the people who do. I'm sure Trump is a more malevolent human being than Zuckerberg, who's apparently a bit weird, but a perfectly okay guy. But with Trump, there's this sense that he's contained in a form that both he and the people around him have a sense of what's going on. But with Zuckerberg, I think he was genuinely surprised to discover what his instrument was being used for, yet he believes his good intentions will make it alright. I think that's scarier. I'm more scared of a well-intentioned person running an out-of-control super machine, which is neither accountable nor actually comprehended by most people, than by a nasty old man in the White House. The nasty old man will be gone relatively soon.

There's a form of irresponsibility which is a form of obliviousness. And Trump is not oblivious. He has a sense of what this is about, and so do his opponents. Just watch the State of the Union. Everyone knows what they're doing. But you can't think of an equivalent to that with Zuckerberg. He occasionally publishes one of his manifestos, and you read it and wonder, what is this?

DC: And he's a relatively young man.

DR: Who might live forever. . . .

Print Citations

CMS: Runciman, David, Charette, Danielle, and Jacob Hamburger. "Democracy's Midlife Crisis: An Interview with David Runciman." In *The Reference Shelf: Democracy Evolving*, edited by Micah L. Issitt, 24-31. Amenia, NY: Grey House Publishing, 2019.

MLA: Runciman, David, Charette, Danielle, and Jacob Hamburger. "Democracy's Midlife Crisis: An Interview with David Runciman." *The Reference Shelf: Democracy Evolving*, edited by Micah L. Issitt, Grey Housing Publishing, 2019, pp. 24-31.

APA: Runciman, D., Charette, D., & Hamburger, J. (2019). Democracy's midlife crisis: An interview with David Runciman. In Micah L. Issitt (Ed.), *The reference shelf: Democracy evolving* (pp. 24-31). Amenia, NY: Grey Housing Publishing.

History and Democracy

By Sean Wilentz

Harvard Magazine, **September-October 2006**

Editor's note: Introducing himself as a Princeton professor wearing a Yale gown as he prepared to address a Harvard audience, historian Sean Wilentz told the new Phi Beta Kappa inductees on June 6 that they had "chosen to reject the old and popular presumption that intelligence imperils, whereas benign stupidity is synonymous with goodness." Having so chosen, "You are pledged to bring the manifold problems of life before your mind while keeping complacency and ideology at bay." Doing so "might help you earn millions of dollars; or help win you recognition, fleeting fame, even immortality; or it might do none of these." Whatever the outcome, "the moral obligation to be intelligent," he said, using Lionel Trilling's words, "always holds."

I have decided to talk about democracy and history because both are matters about which some of the most intelligent people seem confused. As citizens of the world's oldest constitutional democracy, we Americans think we know what the word democracy means. Yet many of us know little about the history of our own democracy, and so our understanding is often cramped. This cramped understanding produces half-baked expectations that the overthrow of tyranny leads directly to democracy. It produces the misleading image of democracy as a panoply of institutions and structures that, once erected, will thrive and then advance democracy's further growth. It produces the conceit that democracy can be easily exported, or that it can be a gift bestowed by benevolent, farseeing rulers, or that it can be won without being fought for, or that its successes are irreversible.

Our own history shows differently. American democracy has been more of an event, a process, than a thing. It occurs when some previously excluded, ordinary persons—what eighteenth-century Americans called "the many"—secure the power not simply to elect their own governors but to oversee the institutions of government, and to criticize those in office. Democracy is nothing without the rule of law, administered by an independent judiciary; yet it is also diminished and threatened when that rule favors one or more portions of the citizenry to the exclusion or even at the expense of the rest.

American democracy is not static. The polity that Alexis de Tocqueville perceived in 1831 as the democratic wave of the future was a polity that included slavery, and excluded from the active citizenry most free black males, all women, and in some places poor white men—hardly a democracy we would recognize today. Yet it was remarkably more democratic than what the framers of the Constitution had in mind only two score and four years before. It is mistaken to judge the democracy of Tocqueville's time too harshly for its partiality and its prejudices, for it was only because of its successes that our own democratic standards can be as lofty as they are.

Above all, democracy is an argument. When Tocqueville visited the United States, democracy in America was the spectacle of Americans arguing over democracy. It still is. The unsettling paradox is that the argument now seems less engaging than it was back then, even though a far larger portion of the population can participate. In 1840, when active citizenship was largely restricted to white men, 80 percent of those citizens voted in the presidential election. Similar rates persisted through the nineteenth century. Today, although we are formally more egalitarian, anything appreciably above 50 percent is considered remarkable. Electoral turnouts are only one indication of democracy's health. But the figures prompt a disturbing question: has the widening of American democracy created countervailing forces which over the long term render the nation's political life less democratic, not more?

The answer might be yes, but I think the situation is also reversible—that the modern equivalents of "the many," wisely led, may rekindle democratic interest and reassert the ideal, expressed by James Madison, that in any proper republic, "the censorial power is in the people over the Government, and not the Government over the people." Perhaps I am wrong, but I vaguely sense such a rekindling around the country, even in this alarming time of genuine danger from without. But much will have to change.

Now, how instructive is the history of our democracy for our democracy's current situation and foreseeable future? As a predictive tool, history is useful mainly in warding off the making of predictions. But history can at least offer what Walt Whitman called, in another context, "themes, hints, provokers."

So much depends on what approach to history one thinks appropriate to democracy, especially American democracy. One popular mode is historical biography. The author of what some regard as the finest Harvard Phi Beta Kappa oration ever, Ralph Waldo Emerson, observed in one of his essays that "there is properly no history; only biography." The phrase is often misread: he was talking not of literary form but of how each of us finds the emphatic facts of history in our private experience. But Emerson did try to render the past through the lives of those he called "Representative Men." Writing biographies of American political leaders has never been out of vogue among either amateur or professional historians. Some have taken Emerson's misunderstood words about history and biography as their motto.

Biography can have major drawbacks if you use it to try and understand American democracy. Too often, biographers try to explain how their subjects embodied, in their deepest character traits, some basic virtue (or bundle of virtues) of the sentimentalized great, gritty, and ultimately good American soul. Political deeds and their consequences, the chief marks of any democratic leader, good or bad, recede before personal rectitude, consistency, daring, and likeability. So do political ideas. Critical engagement with democracy and its discontents gives way to a passive exercise in character appreciation.

Still, biography is essential to understanding democracy's history. Historians who dismiss study of great and powerful individuals as elitist make a small interesting point: the view from the top distorts. But just as political leaders did not create American democracy out of thin air, so the masses of Americans did not simply force their way into the corridors of power. They required leaders, some of the best of whom (and some of the worst) came out of their own ranks.

Another common form of historical writing focuses on ordinary Americans—a style Tocqueville surmised would prevail in democratic America. Especially over the past 30 years, many historians, myself included, have tried to show how the individual and collective experiences of slaves, servants, mechanics, midwives, farmers, and failures illuminated great general trends, in politics as in the rest of American history. It is an infinitely more open and various way of understanding history than traditional biography, and serves, as Tocqueville wrote, "to explain more things in democratic than in aristocratic ages."

Yet to pit the history of the few and the great against that of the many, as some practitioners of both modes recently have, defeats democratic history. It ought to be a truism that, in democratic and undemocratic nations alike, certain individuals have greater influence over history than others. Finally, though, if leaders give democracy's history its shape and tone, they must draw much of their own shape and tone from those they would wish to lead. Neither historical approach is fully intelligible without the other.

What, then, does a democratic history, merging the high and the low and everything in between, offer us? Above all, it affirms that change and contest, sometimes unexpected, are democracy's lifeblood. It shows that, at its most serious, this contest involves Americans, well-known and anonymous, using their moral intelligence to meet fresh exigencies—changing, in the process, not just their political opinions but themselves.

The most astonishing emergence, and convergence, of these themes in American history occurred between 1815 and 1860, when a sizable number of Americans came to regard American slavery no longer as a necessary evil (let alone a positive good) but as an undemocratic enormity that had to be placed as soon as possible on the road to extinction. Pushed, at first, by righteous radicals (who would never gain much of a following), American antislavery faced ferocious opposition, in the North as well as the South. Out of those conflicts arose, in 1854, the first mass antislavery political party in human history, with leaders who often enough had to catch up with their followers—none more so than the Illinois lawyer and hitherto Whig Party hack, Abraham Lincoln.

Forty-five years is a long time, especially in the relatively brief span encompassed by the history of the United States. Yet there are much briefer periods in which it is possible to see American democracy in process of revising itself, one set of democratic conflicts giving way to another. As a historian who deals with concrete events, I'd like to tell a story set in part at this university that illustrates this kind of democratic change.

In 1833, President Andrew Jackson traveled north from Washington to visit, among other places, Harvard, which had decided to grant him the honorary degree of doctor of laws. Jackson had be-

> **We can be reasonably certain that we will be tested by political upheavals we cannot foresee, as the eternal arguing that is the essence of American democracy takes another turn.**

come the head of a popular political force which stood for widened democracy and against privilege. He arrived at Harvard fresh from a triumphant re-election campaign, when he had vetoed the re-chartering of a national bank which had allowed, he said, "the rich and powerful" to "bend the acts of government to their selfish purposes."

Thousands cheered Jackson on his way. (They included a young writer and budding Jacksonian, Nathaniel Hawthorne.) Others, however, thought the entire affair ludicrous. A satirist invented the story that when the unschooled Jackson received his Harvard diploma, he rose, rasped, *"E pluribus unum,* my friends, and *sine qua non,"* and then sat down. And one ashamed member of the Board of Overseers boycotted the ceremony, sickened, he wrote, that his alma mater would entertain "a barbarian who could not write a sentence of grammar and hardly could spell his own name." The Overseer was former president John Quincy Adams, whom Jackson had ejected from the White House in 1828.

Adams was a man of sharp intelligence and enormous learning, but this was not his finest hour. He had come to equate Jackson and the democracy that Jackson advanced with the complete repudiation of learning, liberality, and light. Democracy was on Adams's wrong side, just as he was on the wrong side about democracy. Hawthorne, no barbarian, knew better.

Yet the frame of American democracy was about to change, as the slavery issue soon played havoc with mainstream politics. Two years after his loss to Jackson, Adams had run successfully for a seat in Congress—the only former president to date who has returned to national elected office. And by the mid 1830s, having always steered clear of antislavery politics, Adams suddenly became the leading opponent in the House of Representatives to a new rule that silenced abolitionist petitioners to Congress. Bidden by his constituents as well as his conscience to vindicate democratic freedom of expression, Adams gradually drew closer to the abolitionists.

In July of 1839, a cargo of slaves on the schooner *La Amistad,* sailing from Havana to another part of Cuba, took over the ship and insisted that it be sailed back to Africa, where they had been born, captured, and sold. The *Amistad* was seized by the United States Coast Guard off Long Island, the Africans imprisoned and tried in New Haven for piracy and murder. After the rebels' mostly Yale-educated lawyers succeeded in the lower courts, the case went before the Supreme Court in 1840— and now defending the Africans was John Quincy Adams. "The moment you come, to [the sentence in] the Declaration of Independence, that every man has a right to life and liberty, an inalienable right, this case is decided," Adams told the justices. The Court ruled in the slaves' favor and freed them.

The burden of democracy had shifted. The democratic leader Jackson, who by 1840 had departed the White House, and thought that John Quincy Adams had finally taken leave of his senses, sided with those who insisted that democracy and slavery could go hand in hand. The elitist Adams took another, more egalitarian view, which Abraham Lincoln and others later enlarged into the claim that slavery was democracy's sworn enemy.

As Jackson's own case rather ironically showed, what looks once upon a time like a steely determination to uphold a fixed idea of democracy can turn into an outdated, foolish consistency. With cases like Adams, who adapted to the changing realities of the years, mandarin hauteur can turn into democratic leadership. A great deal depends on the actions of uncelebrated, even lowly persons—including, in this instance, resolute abolitionist petitioners and a band of rebellious slaves. A great deal also depends on an openness, among leaders and followers, to changing course, owning contradictions without becoming their prisoner, and exercising intelligence with a courageous flexibility that is not to be confused with mere opportunism, or convenience, or the pursuit of a career.

None of this history can prescribe how to increase voter interest and turnout. Nor does it present any direct correspondences with current events about which all of us can readily agree. But it does suggest that even when American politics seem permanently cast in a particular shape, when one vision of democracy seems to have supplanted all others, abrupt and shattering changes may well be gathering force. Neither our elected leaders nor ourselves, with all of our intelligence, can know exactly how, or when, or where it will happen. Nor can we be certain that we will like the eventual outcome. But we can be reasonably certain that we will be tested by political upheavals we cannot foresee, as the eternal arguing that is the essence of American democracy takes another turn.

This reasonable certainty brings with it the question of hope, even in the face of tragedy—the kind of hope Lincoln sustained when he proclaimed a rebirth of freedom amid the mass butchery of the Civil War.

The Irish poet and Harvard professor Seamus Heaney writes, in *The Cure at Troy*:

History says, *Don't hope*
On this side of the grave.
But then, once in a lifetime
The longed-for tidal wave
Of justice can rise up,
And hope and history rhyme.

Americans, a hopeful people, like to see democracy, and especially our own democracy, as the quake which causes those infrequent tidal waves of justice—what Thomas Jefferson and Abraham Lincoln both called, decades apart, the world's best hope. But since our history shows that democracy itself is fragile and contested, its meaning eternally fought over, self-satisfaction is as dangerous as it is foolish. And so, if we would make hope and history rhyme, we must force ourselves, with all of our might, to join in democracy's arguments and help write the verse.

Print Citations

CMS: Wilentz, Sean. "History and Democracy." In *The Reference Shelf: Democracy Evolving,* edited by Micah L. Issitt, 32-37. Amenia, NY: Grey House Publishing, 2019.

MLA: Wilentz, Sean. "History and Democracy." *The Reference Shelf: Democracy Evolving,* edited by Micah L. Issitt, Grey Housing Publishing, 2019, pp. 32-37.

APA: Wilentz, S. (2019). History and democracy. In Micah L. Issitt (Ed.), *The reference shelf: Democracy evolving* (pp. 32-37). Amenia, NY: Grey Housing Publishing.

Is the United States of America a Republic or a Democracy?

By Eugene Volokh

The Washington Post, May 15, 2015

I often hear people argue that the United States is a republic, not a democracy. But that's a false dichotomy. A common definition of "republic" is, to quote the *American Heritage Dictionary*, "A political order in which the supreme power lies in a body of citizens who are entitled to vote for officers and representatives responsible to them"—we are that. A common definition of "democracy" is, "Government by the people, exercised either directly or through elected representatives"—we are that, too.

The United States is not a direct democracy, in the sense of a country in which laws (and other government decisions) are made predominantly by majority vote. Some lawmaking is done this way, on the state and local levels, but it's only a tiny fraction of all lawmaking. But we are a representative democracy, which is a form of democracy.

And indeed the American form of government has been called a "democracy" by leading American statesmen and legal commentators from the Framing on. It's true that some Framing-era commentators made arguments that distinguished "democracy" and "republic"; see, for instance, *The Federalist* (No. 10), though even that first draws the distinction between "pure democracy" and a "repub-

> **The United States might be labeled a constitutional federal representative democracy.**

lic," only later just saying "democracy." But even in that era, "representative democracy" was understood as a form of democracy, alongside "pure democracy": John Adams used the term "representative democracy" in 1794; so did Noah Webster in 1785; so did St. George Tucker in his 1803 edition of *Blackstone*; so did Thomas Jefferson in 1815. Tucker's Blackstone likewise uses "democracy" to describe a representative democracy, even when the qualifier "representative" is omitted.

Likewise, James Wilson, one of the main drafters of the Constitution and one of the first Supreme Court Justices, defended the Constitution in 1787 by speaking of the three forms of government being the "monarchical, aristocratical, and democratical," and said that in a democracy the sovereign power is "inherent in the people, and is either exercised by themselves or by their representatives." And Chief Justice John Marshall—who helped lead the fight in the 1788 Virginia Convention for ratifying the U.S. Constitution—likewise defended the Constitution in that convention by describing it as implementing "democracy" (as opposed to "despotism"), and without the need to even add the qualifier "representative."

To be sure, in addition to being a representative democracy, the United States is also a constitutional democracy, in which courts restrain in some measure the democratic will. And the United States is therefore also a constitutional republic. Indeed, the United States might be labeled a constitutional federal representative democracy. But where one word is used, with all the oversimplification that this necessary entails, "democracy" and "republic" both work. Indeed, since direct democracy—again, a government in which all or most laws are made by direct popular vote—would be impractical given the number and complexity of laws that pretty much any state or national government is expected to enact, it's unsurprising that the qualifier "representative" would often be omitted. Practically speaking, representative democracy is the only democracy that's around at any state or national level.

Now one can certainly argue that some aspects of U.S. government should become less direct, and filtered through more layers of representation. One can argue, for instance, that the 17th Amendment should be repealed, and that U.S. senators should no longer be elected directly by the people, but should return to being elected by state legislators who are elected by the people. Or one can argue for repealing state- and local-level initiative and referendum schemes. Or one can argue for making the Electoral College into a deliberative body, in which the electors are supposed to discuss the candidates and make various political deals, rather than being elected solely to vote for particular candidates. And of course one can equally argue for making some aspects of U.S. government more direct, for instance by shifting to truly direct election of the president, or by institute a federal-level initiative and referendum.

But there is no basis for saying that the United States is somehow "not a democracy, but a republic." "Democracy" and "republic" aren't just words that a speaker can arbitrarily define to mean something (e.g., defining democracy as "a form of government in which all laws are made directly by the people"). They are terms that have been given meaning by English speakers more broadly. And both today and in the Framing era, "democracy" has been generally understood to include representative democracy as well as direct democracy.

Print Citations

CMS: Volokh, Eugene. "Is the United States of America a Republic or a Democracy?" In *The Reference Shelf: Democracy Evolving,* edited by Micah L. Issitt, 38-40. Amenia, NY: Grey House Publishing, 2019.

MLA: Volokh, Eugene. "Is the United States of America a Republic or a Democracy?" *The Reference Shelf: Democracy Evolving,* edited by Micah L. Issitt, Grey Housing Publishing, 2019, pp. 38-40.

APA: Volokh, E. (2019). Is the United States of America a republic or a democracy? In Micah L. Issitt (Ed.), *The reference shelf: Democracy evolving* (pp. 38-40). Amenia, NY: Grey Housing Publishing.

Are We Witnessing the Death of Liberal Democracy?

By Ian McKay
The Conversation, May 16, 2019

All over the world, alarm bells are ringing for democracy. Everywhere we find strongmen in charge, enraged citizens and a desperate search for explanations and remedies. Rodrigo Duterte's Philippines. Viktor Orbàn's Hungary. Benjamin Netanyahu's Israel. Maybe something's even going wrong in the United States.

In 1992, political theorist Francis Fukuyama declared there was finally a solution to the riddle: "Who should rule, and why?" The answer: liberal democracy.

A generation later, Fukuyama's declaration is not wearing well.

As it turns out, the structural flaw that would hobble liberal democracy had actually been identified 30 years earlier, in a study called *Possessive Individualism* by University of Toronto political scientist Crawford Brough Macpherson.

He pointed out that liberal democracy was a contradiction in terms. From the 16th century to the 20th, classical liberals of the British tradition had argued for the rights of the "individual." In theory and practice, though, they only counted a person as an individual (almost always male) who had command over himself and his possessions, including human ones.

For all his inspiring words about government created by and responsive to "the people," supposedly liberal philosopher John Locke, investor in the slave trade, had a narrow view of who got to be considered a rights-bearing individual.

The key was property. Society was little more than an agreement among the privileged to respect each other's property rights.

Hardly Pro-democracy

These liberals were not democrats, but after the rise of industrial capitalism, they had to respond to growing populations of working people with their own, often democratic, ideas. Generations of liberals, with John Stuart Mill at the helm, struggled to reconcile their assumptions about free-standing individuals who owned property with the democratic demands of the exploited and excluded.

Until the 1960s, a softer, gentler liberalism seemed to gain ground. The privileges of propertied individuals were preserved, but at a price: welfare programs, unions, public education, housing and health and, worst of all, taxes.

Still, liberals ultimately had to choose between democracy and capitalism. They might find themselves defending both the rights of workers to unionize and of factory owners to fire them, for example. Which should prevail? Macpherson feared the fall-back answer for liberals, whatever their democratic posturing, would often be the owners.

Macpherson's critics painted him as "yesterday's thinker." Didn't he realize, they asked, that liberals had found a sweet spot—harmonizing the public and the private, the people and the propertied, the many and the few?

Macpherson's Prescience

Today, more than three decades after his death, Macpherson's diagnosis—that the acquisitive drive of unfettered capitalism poses a stark challenge to liberty and democracy—seems very prescient.

Liberal democracy has fallen into a world crisis.

Liberal democrats were working to make democracy safe for property, but to their right were hard-nosed businessmen, economists and politicians working on an extreme makeover of liberal democracy that came to be called "neo-liberalism."

Outraged by infringements on capital, determined to roll back socialism and seeing the market as near-infallible, this determined cadre of conservative intellectuals created a movement of reactionary resistance.

Regulations impeding the free flow of capital were demolished. Once-powerful labour movements were eviscerated.

Liberated from effective regulation, financial institutions developed global chains of indebtedness and speculation which, even after the crisis of 2007, have attained pervasive influence.

After three decades of pious liberal hand-wringing, the world is set to warm by three to five degrees Celsius by 2100, a catastrophe attributable to unregulated capitalism.

Liberal Toolbox of No Use

The propertied patterns underlying these civilization-threatening developments cannot be grasped, let alone resisted, using a liberal toolbox.

In the possessive individualism of classical liberalism, we find the seeds of today's democracy crisis. A devotion to property over people is democracy in chains and a planet in peril.

Countless people experience the precariousness wrought by this extreme makeover of the world's liberal order. A neoliberal world, by design, offers minimal security—in employment, social stability, even in reliable networks of knowledge helping us reach reasoned understandings about the world in the company of our fellow citizens.

People longing for security confront, instead, an unintelligible, turbulent world seemingly bent on destroying any prospect of it. Insecurity breeds acute and often angry anxiety. It prompts a search for sanctuary in anti-depressants, opioids and

> **People longing for security confront, instead, an unintelligible, turbulent world seemingly bent on destroying any prospect of it.**

alcohol. A deliberately starved state sector leaves only a few short steps between you and social and economic ruin.

Even the reasoned consideration of factual evidence recedes in a neoliberal world where every institution—newspapers, universities, the state itself—is rethinking itself in neoliberal terms. This very precariousness is represented, not as culturally and psychologically damaging, but as freedom itself.

In this climate, a pervasive culture of militarism offers beleaguered individuals at least the solace of an imagined national community. Our daily work may be regimented, pointless and insecure, but at least we can imagine, beyond it, a world of collective noble endeavour and selfless courage in defence of the nation.

In this militarized culture, many people are plainly looking for strongmen who can stand up for the nation. And around the world, including our corner of it, they're finding them.

Responding to Nationalism

The sovereign political paradox of our time is that a global army of people—precarious, harried, anxious, angry, disenfranchised and above all divested of all social rights to reasonably secure and prosperous livelihoods—is responding avidly to nationalist movements that, on closer inspection, are likely offer them more extreme versions of the hardships they are already enduring.

The Macpherson challenge—to liberate democracy from its neoliberal chains by rethinking property relations right down to their foundations—is daunting, but not unprecedented.

There will be conflict, pain and sacrifice in the long revolution to retrieve democracy and the liberties once sincerely defended by liberals. There will also be excitement and energy. The 21st century is already echoing with cries of dynamic, often youthful participants in such struggles, as they challenge the extreme makeover that has so convulsed contemporary life and placed liberal democracy in question.

They know the hour is late. The stakes could not be higher.

Print Citations

CMS: McKay, Ian. "Are We Witnessing the Death of Liberal Democracy?" In *The Reference Shelf: Democracy Evolving,* edited by Micah L. Issitt, 41-44. Amenia, NY: Grey House Publishing, 2019.

MLA: McKay, Ian. "Are We Witnessing the Death of Liberal Democracy?" *The Reference Shelf: Democracy Evolving,* edited by Micah L. Issitt, Grey Housing Publishing, 2019, pp. 41-44.

APA: McKay, I. (2019). Are we witnessing the death of liberal democracy? In Micah L. Issitt (Ed.), *The reference shelf: Democracy evolving* (pp. 41-44). Amenia, NY: Grey Housing Publishing.

2
Democracy in Context

Although this "Democracy" puzzle sculpture was artist W. F. Herrick's response to the collapse of the Berlin Wall and the dissolution of the Soviet Union, it aptly depicts the difficulty of making any democracy work.

Democratic Identity and Economy

Every aspect of American society is impacted by the perceived health of American democracy and the prevailing interpretation of democratic principles among the American people. This includes such things as the American economy or the way that Americans engage in political discourse, most notably through digital media and the formation of identity groups. Examining these issues helps to illustrate some of the most nuanced threats to the American democratic system as well as the interconnectivity of America's political and economic systems.

Democracy and Capitalism

Writing in a 2018 issue of *Foreign Affairs*, University of Michigan, Ann Arbor professor of political science Yuen Yuen Ang notes, "Most Western observers have long believed that democracy and capitalism go hand in hand, that economic liberalization both requires and propels political liberalization." Yuen argues that this is not the case and provides an example in the development of China, which has become the world's second-largest economy by integrating free market development into their communist political system. China's government calls their system "state capitalism," and it is one example of a growing economic trend, "authoritarian capitalism," in which free-market economic strategies are implemented within authoritarian or dictatorial societies.[1] Proponents of China's state capitalism argue that the imposition of authoritarian controls, while potentially oppressive, enables the state to control the outcome of financial development to a higher degree than is possible in more democratic free market systems.

While authoritarian capitalist states appear to be thriving, there is an increasing perception that America's democratic capitalism is failing. Economists and other experts in the field have identified a number of interrelated problems that threaten American economic prosperity, including difficulty in adjusting to changing technological realities, deepening wealth inequality, and instability of the democratic process itself.

The 2008 financial crisis is the most recent example of America's economic dysfunction. The crisis was largely the result of insufficient regulation on elite financial individuals and institutions. When the economy destabilized, these institutions passed on losses to the public by using massive amounts of tax revenues to avoid collapse. In most cases, the executives of the companies involved actually profited from the recovery, even as most Americans suffered increasing financial instability, in some cases with long-lasting impact. By 2012, as the economy was beginning to recover, the top 10 percent of earners in the United States were collectively earning more than half of the nation's income. The top 1 percent controlled more than 20 percent of the total income in America. This arguably points to structural weaknesses in the American economic system that shield corporate investors, owners, and executives from poor company performance.[2]

A New Gilded Age?

Economic inequality is one of the greatest challenges facing American society in the twenty-first century. The evolution of the American labor market has led to decades of rising income and wealth inequality in which a greater and greater share of wealth is concentrated among the nation's wealthiest families and companies. Over the last century, American productivity has increased and the American economy has grown rapidly, but while wages at the upper end of the income spectrum have continued to rise, at pace with or even outpacing the rate of economic growth, wages for the vast majority of Americans have not increased fast enough to keep pace with the cost of living.[3] Some argue that income inequality results in greater political influence for the wealthy, pushing our democracy into an oligarchy or plutocracy.

The patterns contributing to wealth inequality became increasingly pronounced in the 1980s with the institution of policies that reduced tax burdens on corporations and the wealthy. This was intended to lead to higher productivity and spending, which in turn would result in a flow of resources that would "trickle down" through society. This economic approach remains popular among some conservative politicians despite economic studies demonstrating that it does not work in practice. A 2018 study by the Economic Policy Institute (EPI) found that between 1948 and 1979, productivity in the American economy grew by 103.6 percent, while hourly wages increased by 93.6 percent. During this period, therefore, there was a close link between productivity and profits for American workers. The Republican Party shift away from corporate regulation and taxation changed this pattern, and between 1979 and 2017, though productivity increased by 70.3 percent, hourly compensation increased by only 11.1 percent.[4]

The last time that economic inequality reached such extreme levels was during the "Gilded Age," which lasted from the 1870s to around 1900. One of the most famous industrialists of the era, steel magnate Andrew Carnegie, was quoted in 1892 as saying, "It isn't the man who does the work that makes the money. It's the man who gets other men to do it." Carnegie and the other "robber barons" of that era existed in an economic environment without regulation, in which the political establishment of the day argued, as some politicians still do, that free market competition would ultimately benefit workers. Then, as now, many of those with economic power actively participated in efforts to fight income redistribution. The suppression of hourly wages deepens this pattern, and individuals face extreme challenges when attempting to move to the next income level and typically must expend much or all of their energy simply to keep from falling deeper into financial turmoil.[5]

Disruption and Identity

The Gilded Age was, in part, a reflection of industrialization, a transformative shift in economic realities that left many individuals and entire industries struggling to survive. American society is currently in the grips of a similar disruptive force: digital technology and the digital economy. The ongoing digital revolution is changing the nature of the American economy, ushering out some ways of earning income and introducing others. The digital revolution is closely linked to America's political system as well, as digital technology, like social media, has changed the nature of American political discourse and has altered the ways in which Americans obtain information to guide their political activism and interests. The promise of the Digital Age is that increased communication and increased availability of information can potentially inform and empower consumers, fostering organization and activism. On the other hand, the Digital Age has demonstrated new threats to the integrity of America's democracy. Misinformation and government propagandizing have become more widespread and influential. The proliferation of information has, in some cases, had the opposite effect of that hoped for by the most optimistic analysts of society's technological evolution, creating more insular pockets of the population overwhelmed by data and increasingly nesting within closed information environments.

Another factor driving the evolution of American politics in the twenty-first century is an increase in what has been called "identity politics," a pattern in which individuals embrace political activism based on interests aligning with their particular identity. Identity politics played a major role in the Civil Rights movement of the 1960s as individuals were driven to political activism for the advancement of individuals with whom they shared a specific cultural identity. The Black Power, Chicano Power, Women's Liberation, and LGBTQ rights movements are examples. Modern examples include the #MeToo and Black Lives Matter movements, which are modern continuations of the Civil Rights movements of the 1960s and '70s.

The election of President Donald Trump was strongly motivated by identity politics as well, in this case a manifestation of "white identity" and "white populism." The crystallization of white identity is related to the recognition that white individuals will be a minority in the United States by the mid-twenty-first century. Whereas white individuals once dominated American politics by virtue of their numbers, this will no longer be the case in the next half century, increasing the tendency for voters to embrace whiteness as a core characteristic of their identity and gravitate toward political movements or individuals who promise to preserve this aspect of American culture.[6]

When it comes to the widespread perception of a democratic crisis in the United States, many factors are interconnected. Income inequality and the decline of democratic capitalism is connected to the technological and political disruption of the Digital Age and to the increasingly divisive identity politics of American culture. Every political crisis is in one way or another economic, and every economic crisis is also a matter of politics, social welfare, and identity. It is important, therefore, for Americans to continue to explore the factors contributing to disharmony. Political and social leaders must also promote changes that may foster a greater sense of cohesion, which will in turn lead to a more optimistic future for American democracy.

Works Used

Amadeo, Kimberly. "Income Inequality in America." *The Balance*. Nov 7, 2018. Retrieved from https://www.thebalance.com/income-inequality-in-america-3306190.

Gould, Elise. "Decades of Rising Economic Inequality in the U.S." *EPI*. Economic Policy Institute. Mar 27, 2019. Retrieved from https://www.epi.org/publication/decades-of-rising-economic-inequality-in-the-u-s-testimony-before-the-u-s-house-of-representatives-ways-and-means-committee/.

Huyssen, David. "We Won't Get Out of the Second Gilded Age the Way We Got Out of the First." *Vox*. Apr 1, 2019. Retrieved from https://www.vox.com/first-person/2019/4/1/18286084/gilded-age-income-inequality-robber-baron.

Illing, Sean. "White Identity Politics Is about More Than Racism." *Vox*. Apr 27, 2019. Retrieved from https://www.vox.com/2019/4/26/18306125/white-identity-politics-trump-racism-ashley-jardina.

Lopez, German. "The Battle over Identity Politics, Explained." *Vox*. Aug 17, 2017. Retrieved from https://www.vox.com/identities/2016/12/2/13718770/identity-politics.

Rothman, Lily. "How American Inequality in the Gilded Age Compares to Today." *Time*. Feb 5, 2018. Retrieved from http://time.com/5122375/american-inequality-gilded-age/.

Rudd, Kevin. "The Rise of Authoritarian Capitalism." *The New York Times*. Sep 16, 2018. Retrieved from https://www.nytimes.com/2018/09/16/opinion/politics/kevin-rudd-authoritarian-capitalism.html.

Yuen Yuen Ang. "Autocracy with Chinese Characteristics." *Foreign Affairs*. May/June 2018. Retrieved from https://www.foreignaffairs.com/articles/asia/2018-04-16/autocracy-chinese-characteristics.

Notes

1. Yuen Yuen Ang, "Autocracy with Chinese Characteristics."
2. Rudd, "The Rise of Authoritarian Capitalism."
3. Amadeo, "Income Inequality in America."
4. Gould, "Decades of Rising Economic Inequality in the U.S."
5. Rothman, "How American Inequality in the Gilded Age Compares to Today."
6. Illing, "White Identity Politics Is about More Than Racism."

The Rise of Authoritarian Capitalism

By Kevin Rudd

The New York Times, September 16, 2018

Liberal democracy and capitalism have been the two commanding political and economic ideas of Western history since the 19th century. Now, however, the fate of these once-galvanizing global principles is increasingly uncertain.

Democratic capitalism is showing signs of deep, systemic sickness in the United States, Europe and Australasia, even as varieties of state or authoritarian capitalism are slowly becoming entrenched around the world, particularly in China and Russia.

In the developing world, democratic capitalism has always had a mixed reputation. While the West preached its freedoms at home, it happily engaged in political and economic exploitation abroad. The hypocrisy of colonialism is still lost on many in the West, who ask why so many people in the developing world have found the truths of Western political and economic freedom to be less than self-evident in their own national experiences.

Nevertheless, there is something elementally powerful about the underlying idea of individual dignity and freedom. Despite the baggage of colonialism, democratic capitalism succeeded remarkably in Asia, Africa and Latin America after World War II, and after the Cold War in particular. The democracy watchdog group Freedom House reports that as of 2017, 88 of 195 states were classified as "free," compared with 65 of 165 in 1990.

After the end of the Cold War, however, four structural challenges emerged to endanger the future of democratic capitalism: financial instability, technological disruption, widening social and economic inequality and structural weaknesses in democratic politics. If the West cannot overcome these challenges, they will, over time, spread to the rest of the world and undermine open polities, economies and societies.

The 2008 financial crisis, one sign of a systemic sickness, occurred because of poorly regulated financial elites. The costs to governments and peoples were bailouts, lost jobs and more public debt. Governments had to scramble to save capitalism from itself as financial markets failed to self-correct. As a result, the markets privatized their profits and socialized their losses. Only one top bank executive went to jail. The taxpayer, by and large, paid the bill. And democratically elected governments were routinely tossed out because they had either failed to prevent the crisis, or were unable to manage the resulting public debt—or both. Another crisis could push the system to its breaking point. Yet a weakened Dodd-Frank Act in the United States now makes a repeat of the 2008 crisis more likely. All at a time when governments have even less room to respond.

Revolutions in technology threaten democracies' ability to cope with the complexity, speed and trajectory of change. Democracies, like corporations, can now be hacked. Social media distorts the free flow of facts that has been the lifeblood of democratic capitalism. In the past, disruptions to employment brought about by rapid technological change resulted in a movement of lower-skilled jobs to newer industries. But now we may no longer be capable of providing enough new jobs in areas where they are needed.

The financial and technological challenges are compounded by a rising economic inequality. The extreme concentration of wealth in the United States in recent decades is well documented. The new barons of capital and technology thrive while the American middle class stagnates and the American dream fades. The bottom line is simple: Citizens will continue to support their democratic capitalist systems so long as there is reasonable equality of opportunity and a humane social safety net. Take these away and the citizenry no longer has a material stake in mainstream democratic politics. Nationalism and xenophobia take over.

> **Citizens will continue to support their democratic capitalist systems so long as there is reasonable equality of opportunity and a humane social safety net.**

Lastly, there are the inherent structural failings in modern democratic politics. In the United States, unrestricted campaign financing continues to undermine democracy. The spectacular corruption of the electoral redistricting system—gerrymandering—only compounds the problem. On top of this, the polarization of traditional news media by Fox News and others is poisoning the capacity of the democratic system to build a sustainable consensus around what is left of the political center, as shown by the debacle of the American gun-control debate.

As Western democracies look increasingly sick, other systems of governance are now on offer. Russian nationalism represents a departure from Western political, economic and diplomatic norms. China has become increasingly confident in its own model, described as authoritarian or state capitalism. And its "Beijing consensus" is held up to the non-Western world as an example of a more effective form of national, and even international, governance.

If the United States wants to remain a global beacon of democratic capitalism, it must first confront its domestic challenges. The American social contract needs to be rebuilt through a revised New Deal. The social impact of technological change must be politically managed, rather than left to the market. Finance should return to its historical role as the servant of the real economy, rather than its master. And the Supreme Court must set a new direction on campaign finance (by overturning the Citizens United decision), gerrymandering and some of the crazier interpretations of the Second Amendment used to justify a breakdown in basic law and order.

The United States also needs to re-embrace its responsibilities to the liberal international order it painstakingly created after World War II. This order was anchored in the United Nations Charter, the Universal Declaration of Human Rights, the General Agreement on Tariffs and Trade, the International Monetary Fund and other institutions and principles that have become the bedrock of free societies, free economies and free polities. The world now asks: Does the United States still embrace this order?

Both democracy and capitalism are relatively recent developments in the long history of the West. They represent even more recent developments in the considerably longer history of the East. Both represent the enduring idea of freedom. Yet both rest on increasingly fragile political and economic institutions. History cautions us against any belief that democratic capitalism will somehow inevitably prevail. Unless, of course, we make it so by tending the garden while there is still time.

Print Citations

CMS: Rudd, Kevin. "The Rise of Authoritarian Capitalism." In *The Reference Shelf: Democracy Evolving,* edited by Micah L. Issitt, 51-53. Amenia, NY: Grey House Publishing, 2019.

MLA: Rudd, Kevin. "The Rise of Authoritarian Capitalism." *The Reference Shelf: Democracy Evolving,* edited by Micah L. Issitt, Grey Housing Publishing, 2019, pp. 51-53.

APA: Rudd, K. (2019). The rise of authoritarian capitalism. In Micah L. Issitt (Ed.), *The reference shelf: Democracy evolving* (pp. 51-53). Amenia, NY: Grey Housing Publishing.

Big Fail: The Internet Hasn't Helped Democracy

By Robert Diab

The Conversation, October 15, 2018

Hardly a week goes by without news of another data breach at a large corporation affecting millions, most recently Facebook.

In 2016, the issue became political with evidence of Russian interference in the U.S. election and the spectre of foreign control over public opinion.

American lawmakers called on Facebook's CEO to account in high-profile congressional hearings, but the discussion focused mainly on privacy and personal data.

We have yet to come to terms with the staggering degree of control the major platforms exercise over political speech and what it means for democracy.

A new book on the economics of attention online urges us to do so. It shows that more and more of our public conversation is unfolding within a dwindling coterie of sites that are controlled by a small few, largely unregulated and geared primarily to profit rather than public interest.

False Earlier Assumptions about the Net

In the recently published *The Internet Trap: How the Digital Economy Builds Monopolies and Undermined Democracy* author and professor Matthew Hindman suggests that as we enter the web's third decade, market forces drive the vast majority of traffic and profit to an exceedingly small group of sites, with no change on the horizon.

Hindman's findings unsettle an earlier picture of the web as a tool for broader civic engagement and a healthier democracy—a view prominently associated with Harvard's Yochai Benkler.

In his 2006 book *The Wealth of Networks*, Benkler noted that in the industrial age, one could only reach a wider audience by making "ever-larger investments in physical capital"—for example in telegraphs, presses, radio and TV transmitters—ensuring a corporate monopoly over public speech.

But with digital networks enabling anyone to reach millions of people for virtually nothing, the public sphere was sure to become more accessible, diverse and robust. Others were equally bullish.

In the 2008 book *Here Comes Everybody*, Clay Shirky saw the new terrain fostering a "mass amateurization" of cultural and political engagement.

Reality Was Less Rosy

Yet, as Hindman wrote in 2008 in *The Myth of Digital Democracy*, the blogosphere did not result in a great dispersal of attention or a big increase in audience diversity. By decade's end, news and political organizations online remained highly concentrated.

James Webster corroborated this view in 2014's *The Marketplace of Attention*, showing that greater diversity and polarization on the web had been "overstated." The long online tail stretches far, he noted, but few tend to dwell for long in the "sanctuaries" at its extremes.

In *The Internet Trap*, Hindman extends the inquiry, finding that while the net does lower the basic cost of mass communication, the cost of building and keeping a large audience remains high.

Studying the rise of sites like Google and Amazon, Hindman found that the net's most popular sites built and maintained their audiences by harnessing "a host of economies of scale" that go beyond network effects.

Popular sites have the staff and resources to ensure their sites "load faster," "are prettier and more usable" and "have more content updated more frequently." Their users are "more practised in navigating" their sites and return more often, boosting their search rankings and ad revenue.

What It Means for News and Political Speech

We often assume small newspapers "have a revenue problem, not a readership problem." Hindman shows they have both. Tracking some 250,000 users in the "100 largest local media markets" in the United States, he found that local news sites garner roughly one-sixth of news traffic, and "just one-half of one per cent of traffic overall."

> **More of our public conversation is unfolding within a dwindling coterie of sites that are controlled by a small few, largely unregulated and geared primarily to profit rather than public interest.**

The smaller players online are thus becoming ever more marginal to the larger political conversation. Hindman counsels them to build stickier sites—less cluttered, faster to load, fresher.

But his findings suggest it may not be that simple.

Hindman's work points to a future where a few sites exert an outsized influence over public debate, raising a host of concerns.

Russian interference in another major election by hacking a hugely popular platform like Facebook is obviously one of them.

More crucially, as British historian Mark Mazower notes, the near-monopoly over attention online by Facebook and other large sites threatens democracy by constraining conversation in terms of "profits not politics."

The large portals encourage "instant gratification, when democracy presupposes a capacity for frustration and patience." As Mazower writed: "Populism is the natural condition of democratic politics in the age of Twitter."

If our picture of the web as a tool for citizen empowerment is a mostly a mirage, it's time we regulated the dominant sites more effectively in order to serve the public interest.

Print Citations

CMS: Diab, Robert. "Big Fail: The Internet Hasn't Helped Democracy." In *The Reference Shelf: Democracy Evolving,* edited by Micah L. Issitt, 54-56. Amenia, NY: Grey House Publishing, 2019.

MLA: Diab, Robert. "Big Fail: The Internet Hasn't Helped Democracy." *The Reference Shelf: Democracy Evolving,* edited by Micah L. Issitt, Grey Housing Publishing, 2019, pp. 54-56.

APA: Diab, R. (2019). Big fail: The internet hasn't helped democracy." In Micah L. Issitt (Ed.), *The reference shelf: Democracy evolving* (pp. 54-56). Amenia, NY: Grey Housing Publishing.

American Democracy Is Ailing: Thinking Like an Economist Can Help

By Gary Saul Morson and Morton Schapiro
The Washington Post, April 10, 2019

There is a Latin saying that was favored by 19th-century revolutionaries: *Fiat justitia, et pereat mundus*. "Let justice be done, though the world perish."

That is not an economist's way of thinking, but it does seem to be how competing groups of ideologues and moralists increasingly view decision-making.

Consider policies advocated by many on the left or the right about issues they care about most deeply, and it soon becomes apparent that they are thinking not practically, but almost theologically—unable to tolerate compromise, unwilling to consider trade-offs.

Economics is all about the allocation of scarce resources. There are no gains without costs. Is one really prepared to let the world perish rather than allow the smallest injustice?

Moralists don't perform cost-benefit analyses designed to reduce the most sin with the least effort. They don't think of trade-offs among the Ten Commandments. Their worldview militates against such thinking, which for them carries a whiff of the devil's sulfur.

With politics becoming a secular religion, and its practitioners taking similarly inflexible stands, affording little discernible benefit to the nation, it might be worthwhile to consider how an economist would approach some of the vital issues today.

In understanding people's preferences, economists consider not what they say but what they do—their "revealed preferences." Many today believe, with justification, that carbon use and climate change pose an imminent, existential threat to the planet. Yet if one reflexively opposes nuclear power or fracking and the natural gas it produces, all of which can reduce carbon emissions even if they are themselves not perfectly green, can one really believe in imminent global catastrophe, or is one thinking like a moralist who will not choose one sin over another?

The Green New Deal, endorsed by several Democratic presidential candidates, proposes to phase out internal-combustion engines and retrofit all buildings in the United States over a short time. But the deal's proponents also call for guaranteed jobs along with suitable housing and healthy food for all, while ensuring that eminent domain is not abused. Surely, if the planet faces a climate emergency, one should postpone such causes, however desirable. Insisting on addressing all problems at once means that none is particularly urgent.

Scarcity exists, and imperfect choices must be made. Great literature, as well as great economics, has illustrated this truth. Anton Chekhov repeatedly criticized the self-indulgence of those failing to allocate time, money and energy effectively. For him, high-minded waste is never desirable. Fyodor Dostoevsky, in *The Brothers Karamazov*, portrays Ivan and Alyosha as high-mindedly agreeing that they would not save millions of children if it meant sacrificing even one of them. Is that really humane?

> **Neither protectionism, nor free trade without any provision for worker retraining or support, holds much sway with economists in most nations.**

The fact is that we can identify approaches more likely to be effective in attaining good goals—and so are justified ethically as well as practically. In topic after topic, there is a surprisingly robust, data-backed consensus among economists to guide us.

For example, while the right has a proclivity for lowering tax rates and the left for raising them, economists understand general principles based on estimating trade-offs. A maximum marginal tax rate of, say, 20 percent, would be as misguided as, say, one of 80 percent.

Or consider the minimum wage. Just as eliminating it would hurt many workers, raising it too much would reduce employment opportunities for precisely those in greatest need of them. Today, most American economists favor a range between $12 and $15 an hour. Go far above or below these numbers and the harm will far outweigh the good.

How about trade policy? Neither protectionism, nor free trade without any provision for worker retraining or support, holds much sway with economists in most nations. A portion of the overall gains from free trade could be used to mitigate harm to those whom it hurts, and the country would still come out ahead.

As glaciers melt, wealth inequality rises and debt balloons, it's time for a recommitment to prudence—and to pursuing workable policies instead of staking out impossible positions on the left or the right.

The great challenge for economists today is to find new and better ways to make their cases, with the goal of kindling a general appreciation of essential economic ideas such as incentives, trade-offs, marginal utility and revealed preferences. Learning to practice the dispassionate analysis of data would be helpful, too. Citizens making informed choices are good for the health of democracy, and lately American democracy has been ailing.

Print Citations

CMS: Morson, Gary Saul, and Morton Shapiro. "American Democracy Is Ailing: Thinking Like an Economist Can Help." In *The Reference Shelf: Democracy Evolving,* edited by Micah L. Issitt, 57-59. Amenia, NY: Grey House Publishing, 2019.

MLA: Morson, Gary Saul, and Morton Shapiro. "American Democracy Is Ailing: Thinking Like an Economist Can Help." *The Reference Shelf: Democracy Evolving,* edited by Micah L. Issitt, Grey Housing Publishing, 2019, pp. 57-59.

APA: Morson, G.S., & Shapiro, M. (2019). American democracy is ailing: Thinking like an economist can help. In Micah L. Issitt (Ed.), *The reference shelf: Democracy evolving* (pp. 57-59). Amenia, NY: Grey Housing Publishing.

Economic Freedom Is Essential to Democracy

By William Dunkelberg
Forbes, June 6, 2018

The strength of a democracy depends on the economic and political freedom of its citizens. Compare the strength of economies and the welfare of citizens that are democracies to those that are directed by despotic regimes—it's clear. But even in a democracy, there is a "tyrant" that can exercise despotic power if left unchecked— the government: federal, state and local. Government policies can restrict freedom of choice, confiscate resources and valuable time, compel actions that grossly fail to pass any cost-benefit test, show favoritism, and enforce servitude. And these powers can be used to entrench a political dynasty. Political freedom and the right to express views openly as well as to vote free of coercion are critical, but economic freedom, the right to use the fruits of our labor every day without political influence, is essential for democracy to thrive.

America's small businesses employ half our private sector workers, produce nearly half of our private sector output, and are routinely praised by politicians for their importance. But these politicians frequently limit the economic freedom of small businesses. The top problems (out of a list of 75) facing these firms according to NFIB's Small Business Problems and Priorities poll of a sample of its hundreds of thousands of member firms are:

1. Cost of health insurance
2. Unreasonable government regulations
3. Federal taxes on business income
4. Uncertainty over economic conditions
5. Tax complexity
6. Uncertainty over government actions
7. Frequent changes in federal tax laws and rules
8. Property taxes
9. State taxes on business income

Small business owners' top problems are clear evidence of the reach of government into the economic freedom of private economic agents.

The current administration has taken several steps to support a healthier democracy. Regulatory burdens are being reduced, with government playing a smaller role in directing the use of our valuable capital. Lower compliance costs mean more funds available to invest in the firm's growth, providing more jobs and better incomes for citizens. The new tax code is returning

> **Economic freedom, the right to use the fruits of our labor every day without political influence, is essential for democracy to thrive.**

money to the private sector where history makes clear it will be better invested than by a government bureaucracy. The misuse of government for political purposes is being exposed and improvements will be made. Protecting our democracy requires that the private sector not be deprived of its right to manage its economic affairs, and the process of "delevering" governments grip on the private sector is underway. History has proven that governments cannot deliver the success that an unfettered economy can.

There is much more work to be done. Rising health insurance costs have not been addressed, and tax code complexity remains an obstacle for small business owners. Governments have made promises (pensions, welfare, etc.) that cannot be met without a heavy tax on the private sector. The rising burden of our debt will weigh heavily on the private sector, siphoning off resources to pay interest to our lenders. Economic growth is critical to our ability to deal with these issues. The economy is now growing 50 percent faster than it did from 2009-16, producing more jobs, income, and of course tax revenue, not from higher tax rates but a growing tax base and rising employment. Combined with more sensible regulation, growth will better prepare us to deal with our economic and political problems and preserve and strengthen our democracy.

Print Citations

CMS: Dunkelberg, William. "Economic Freedom Is Essential to Democracy." In *The Reference Shelf: Democracy Evolving,* edited by Micah L. Issitt, 60-61. Amenia, NY: Grey House Publishing, 2019.

MLA: Dunkelberg, William. "Economic Freedom Is Essential to Democracy." *The Reference Shelf: Democracy Evolving,* edited by Micah L. Issitt, Grey Housing Publishing, 2019, pp. 60-61.

APA: Dunkelberg, W. (2019). Economic freedom is essential to democracy. In Micah L. Issitt (Ed.), *The reference shelf: Democracy evolving* (pp. 60-61). Amenia, NY: Grey Housing Publishing.

E Pluribus Unum? The Fight Over Identity Politics

By Stacey Y. Abrams; John Sides, Michael Tesler, and Lynn
Vavreck; Jennifer A. Richeson; and Francis Fukuyama
Foreign Affairs, March/April 2019

IDENTITY POLITICS STRENGTHENS DEMOCRACY

Stacey Y. Abrams

Recent political upheavals have reinvigorated a long-running debate about the role of identity in American politics—and especially American elections. Electoral politics have long been a lagging indicator of social change. For hundreds of years, the electorate was limited by laws that explicitly deprived women, African Americans, and other groups of the right to vote. (Efforts to deny voting rights and suppress voter turnout continue today, in less overt forms but with the same ill intent.) When marginalized groups finally gained access to the ballot, it took time for them to organize around opposition to the specific forms of discrimination and mistreatment that continued to plague them—and longer still for political parties and candidates to respond to such activism. In recent decades, however, rapid demographic and technological changes have accelerated this process, bolstering demands for inclusion and raising expectations in communities that had long been conditioned to accept a slow pace of change. In the past decade, the U.S. electorate has become younger and more ethnically diverse. Meanwhile, social media has changed the political landscape. Facebook captures examples of inequality and makes them available for endless replay. Twitter links the voiceless to newsmakers. Instagram immortalizes the faces and consequences of discrimination. Isolated cruelties are yoked into a powerful narrative of marginalization that spurs a common cause.

These changes have encouraged activists and political challengers to make demands with a high level of specificity—to take the identities that dominant groups have used to oppress them and convert them into tools of democratic justice. Critics of this phenomenon, including Francis Fukuyama ("Against Identity Politics," September/October 2018), condemn it as the practice of "identity politics." But Fukuyama's criticism relies on a number of misjudgments. First, Fukuyama complains that "again and again, groups have come to believe that their identities—whether national, religious, ethnic, sexual, gender, or otherwise—are not receiving adequate recognition." In the United States, marginalized groups have indeed come to believe this—because it is true. Fukuyama also warns that Americans are fragmenting "into segments based on ever-narrower identities, threatening the possibility of deliberation and collective action by society as a whole." But what Fukuyama laments as "fracturing" is in reality the result of marginalized groups finally overcoming centuries-long efforts to erase them from the American polity—activism that will strengthen democratic rule, not threaten it.

The Class Trap

Fukuyama claims that the Democratic Party "has a major choice to make." The party, he writes, can continue "doubling down on the mobilization of the identity groups that today supply its most fervent activists: African Americans, Hispanics, professional women, the LGBT community, and so on." Or it can take Fukuyama's preferred tack, focusing more on economic issues in an attempt to "win back some of the white working-class voters . . . who have defected to the Republican Party in recent elections."

Fukuyama and other critics of identity politics contend that broad categories such as economic class contain multitudes and that all attention should focus on wide constructs rather than the substrates of inequality. But such arguments fail to acknowledge that some members of any particular economic class have advantages not enjoyed by others in their cohort. U.S. history abounds with examples of members of dominant groups abandoning class solidarity after concluding that opportunity is a zero-sum game. The oppressed have often aimed their impotent rage at those too low on the social scale to even attempt rebellion. This is particularly true in the catchall category known as "the working class." Conflict between black and white laborers stretches back to the earliest eras in U.S. history, which witnessed tensions between African slaves and European indentured servants. Racism and sexism have long tarnished the heroic story of the U.S. labor movement—defects that contributed to the rise of a segregated middle class and to persistent pay disparities between men and women, disparities exacerbated by racial differences. Indeed, the American working class has consistently relied on people of color and women to push for improved status for workers but has been slow to include them in the movement's victories.

The facile advice to focus solely on class ignores these complex links among American notions of race, gender, and economics. As Fukuyama himself notes, it has been difficult "to create broad coalitions to fight for redistribution," since "members of the working class who also belong to higher-status identity groups (such as whites in the United States) tend to resist making common cause with those below them, and vice versa." Fukuyama's preferred strategy is also called into question by the success that the Democratic Party enjoyed in 2018 by engaging in what he derides as identity politics. Last year, I was the Democratic Party's gubernatorial nominee in Georgia and became the first African American woman in U.S. history to be nominated for governor by a major political party. In my bid for office, I intentionally and vigorously highlighted communities of color and other marginalized groups, not to the exclusion of others but as a recognition of their specific policy needs. My campaign championed reforms to eliminate police shootings of African Americans, protect the LGBTQ community against ersatz religious freedom legislation, expand Medicaid to save rural hospitals, and reaffirm that undocumented immigrants deserve legal protections. I refused to accept the notion that the voters most affected by these policies would invariably support me simply because I was a member of a minority group. (The truth is that when people do not hear their causes authentically addressed by campaigns, they generally just don't vote at all.) My campaign built an unprecedented coalition of people of color, rural whites, suburban dwellers, and young people in the Deep South by articulating an understanding of each group's unique concerns instead of trying to create a false image of universality. As a result, in a midterm contest with a record-high turnout of nearly four million voters, I received more votes than any Democrat in Georgia's history, falling a scant 54,000 votes shy of victory in a contest riddled with voting irregularities that benefited my opponent.

Different Strokes

Beyond electoral politics, Fukuyama and others argue that by calling out ethnic, cultural, gender, or sexual differences, marginalized groups harm themselves and their causes. By enumerating and celebrating distinctions, the argument goes, they give their opponents reasons for further excluding them. But minorities and the marginalized have little choice but to fight against the particular methods of discrimination employed against them. The marginalized did not create identity politics: their identities have been forced on them by dominant groups, and politics is the most effective method of revolt.

To seek redress and inclusion, the first step is to identify the barriers to entry: an array of laws and informal rules to proscribe, diminish, and isolate the marginalized. The specific methods by which the United States has excluded women, Native Americans, African Americans, immigrants, and the LGBTQ community from property ownership, educational achievement, and political enfranchisement have differed; so, too, have the most successful methods of fighting for inclusion—hence the need for a politics that respects and reflects the complicated nature of these identities and the ways in which they intersect. The basis for sustainable progress is legal protections grounded in an awareness of how identity has been used to deny opportunity. The LGBTQ community is not included in civil rights protections, which means members may lose their jobs or their right to housing or adoption. Antiabortion rules disproportionately harm women of color and low-income women of every ethnicity, affecting their economic capacity and threatening their very lives. Voter suppression, the most insidious tool to thwart the effectiveness of identity politics, demands the renewal of the Voting Rights Act of 1965 and massive reforms at the state and local levels.

When the groups most affected by these issues insist on acknowledgment of their intrinsic difference, it should not be viewed as divisive. Embracing the distinct histories and identities of groups in a democracy enhances the complexity and capacity of the whole. For example, by claiming the unique attributes of woman-hood—and, for women of color, the experience of inhabiting the intersection of marginalized gender and race—feminists have demonstrated how those characteristics could be leveraged to enhance the whole. Take, for example, the Family and Medical Leave Act, which feminists originally pushed for in order to guarantee women's right to give birth and still keep their jobs, but which men have also come to rely on to take time off from work to care for children or aging parents.

The current demographic and social evolution toward diversity in the United States has played out alongside a trend toward greater economic and social inequality. These parallel but distinct developments are inextricably bound together. The entrance of the marginalized into the workplace, the commons, and the body politic—achieved through litigation and legislation—spawned reactionary limits on their legal standing and restrictions meant to block their complaints and prevent remedies. The natural antidote to this condition is not a retrenchment to amorphous, universal descriptors devoid of context or nuance. Instead, Americans must thoughtfully pursue an expanded, identity-conscious politics. New, vibrant, noisy voices represent the strongest tool to manage the growing pains of multicultural coexistence. By embracing identity and its prickly, uncomfortable contours, Americans will become more likely to grow as one.

Stacey Y. Abrams served as Minority Leader of the Georgia House of Representatives from 2011 to 2017 and was the Democratic Party's nominee in Georgia's 2018 gubernatorial election.

IDENTITY POLITICS CAN LEAD TO PROGRESS

John Sides, Michael Tesler, and Lynn Vavreck

Francis Fukuyama argues that "identity politics has become a master concept that explains much of what is going on in global affairs." He attributes a variety of political developments in the United States and abroad—especially the emergence of populist nationalism—to identity politics. In Fukuyama's telling, the rise of identity politics constitutes a fall from grace. For him, most of "twentieth-century politics was defined by economic issues." But in the 1960s, he writes, the civil rights, feminist, and other social movements embraced identity politics. Later, he claims, forces on the political right followed suit, adopting "language and framing from the left." Fukuyama warns that if democratic societies continue "fracturing into segments based on ever-narrower identities," the result will be "state breakdown and, ultimately, failure."

Identity is indeed a "master concept" for understanding American politics. But identity politics has a much longer history than Fukuyama describes. And in the United States, identity politics hasn't led to the breakdown of democracy; rather, it has helped democracy thrive.

Origin Story

In Fukuyama's telling, identity politics first emerged in the second half of the twentieth century. In fact, Americans have been engaged in identity politics since the founding of the republic. If the fight for civil rights for African Americans was fueled by identity politics, then so was the fight to establish and ensure white supremacy via slavery and Jim Crow. In other words, identity politics isn't behind only the efforts of marginalized groups to seek redress: it also drives the efforts of dominant groups to marginalize others.

Fukuyama believes identity politics went too far when groups such as African Americans began to "assert a separate identity" and "demand respect for [their members] as different from the mainstream society." Leaving aside whether that statement correctly characterizes the goal of such groups, it is important to acknowledge that identity politics also defined who was and who was not part of "mainstream society" in the first place.

In Fukuyama's telling, U.S. politics were healthier when Americans—especially those on the left—organized around economic concerns that transcended ethnic categories. "In past eras," he writes, "progressives appealed to a shared experience of exploitation and resentment of rich capitalists." But there is no period in U.S. history when economics were so cleanly divorced from identity. For example, as the political scientist Ira Katznelson has documented, the key social welfare programs of the New Deal era were predicated on racial discrimination: U.S. President Franklin Roosevelt relied on the support of white segregationists, which he won by allowing southern states to prevent blacks from enjoying the New Deal's benefits. Identity, and especially racial and ethnic identity, has always been intrinsic to fights over economic opportunity and equality.

This is not to say that today's identity politics is the same as its historical forebears. What makes it different is how tightly Americans' views about racial, ethic, and religious identities are now bound up with another salient American identity: partisan affiliation. Well before 2016, Democratic and Republican voters had begun to diverge in their views of immigration and racial equality. Democrats became more supportive of immigration and more willing to attribute racial inequality to discrimination. Republicans became less supportive of immigration and more willing to attribute racial inequality to a lack of effort on the part of African Americans. This divergence sharpened during Barack Obama's candidacy and presidency, as whites' racial attitudes became more closely tied to their partisan identities.

This trend might have accelerated even faster than it did had major political leaders tried to exploit it. But Obama actually talked about race less than other recent Democratic presidents and frequently used rhetoric that sought to unify Americans of different racial backgrounds. Meanwhile, Obama's Republican opponents in the presidential elections of 2008 and 2012, John McCain and Mitt Romney, chose not to stoke racialized fears of Obama.

Donald Trump was different. His provocative statements about race, immigration, and Islam helped define the 2016 election. Partly as a result, Americans' views on such issues became stronger predictors of how they voted. For example, compared with in earlier elections, it was easier to determine how people voted in 2016 based on whether they wanted a pathway to citizenship for undocumented immigrants or believed that racial inequality was just a matter of minorities "not trying hard enough." Meanwhile, economic issues achieved more political potency when refracted through race. As far back as the 2016 Republican primary, whether voters supported Trump depended less on whether they were worried about losing their own jobs than it did on whether they were worried about whites losing jobs to ethnic minorities.

Whose Choice?

Since the election, this alignment of partisanship and attitudes about race and immigration has grown even stronger, and it has an important implication for Fukuyama's argument. Fukuyama's favored political agenda closely resembles that of Democratic voters and the Democratic Party. He supports remedies for police violence against minorities and the sexual harassment of women, endorses birthright citizenship, and wants an American identity based on ideals rather than on "blood and soil" nationalism.

The most forceful opposition to such ideas has come from the Trump administration and its Republican allies and supporters. Yet Fukuyama does not put the onus on Republicans to reject Trump. In his view, the "major choice" belongs to the Democratic Party, which must decide whether to double down on "the mobilization of . . . identity groups" or "try to win back some of the white working-class voters . . . who have defected" to the GOP. But if Fukuyama wants federal action on his policy agenda in an era of divided government and narrow congressional majorities, the real onus is on Republicans to support his ideas. And if he wants an American identity based on shared values and open to all citizens—even those who hail from what Trump reportedly called "shithole countries"—then he will need at least some Republicans to stand up to Trump.

Fukuyama may be against identity politics, but identity politics is also critical to the success of the agenda that he supports. History has shown that progress toward equality doesn't come about because of happenstance, a sudden change of heart on Capitol Hill, or the magnanimity of dominant groups. Instead, progress comes when marginalized groups organize around their shared identities. Their fight is often unpopular. In one 1964 survey, conducted a few months after the passage of the Civil Rights Act, of those polled, 84 percent of southerners and 64 percent of Americans living outside the South said that civil rights leaders were pushing too fast. But pushing was their only recourse, and pushing helped change the country's laws and attitudes.

Fukuyama wants a unifying American identity, what he calls a "creedal national identity." But the country is already fairly close to having one. According to the December 2016 Views of the Electorate Research, or VOTER, Survey, 93 percent of Americans think that respecting U.S. political institutions and laws is somewhat or very important to "being American." Far fewer believe that it's important to be born in the United States (55 percent) or to have European heritage (20 percent).

Moreover, most Americans actually place identity politics at the center of the American creed: the vast majority (88 percent) think that accepting people of diverse racial and religious backgrounds is important to being American.

There is no necessary tension between identity politics and the American creed. The question is whether identity politics will help Americans live up to that creed. Historically, it has.

John Sides, Michael Tesler, and Lynn Vavreck are political scientists and the authors of Identity Crisis: The 2016 Presidential Campaign and the Battle for the Meaning of America.

A CREEDAL IDENTITY IS NOT ENOUGH

Jennifer A. Richeson

Francis Fukuyama argues that identity politics is eroding national unity in the United States and Europe, undermining the kind of civil discourse essential to the maintenance of liberal democracy. He also claims that "perhaps the worst thing about identity politics as currently practiced by the left is that it has stimulated the rise of identity politics on the right." This is highly misleading. Identity politics was part of the American political discourse long before liberals and leftists began to practice it in the 1960s and 1970s. Think of the anti-immigrant Know-Nothing Party in the 1850s and the white-supremacist Ku Klux Klan during the first half of the twentieth century. What were such groups if not early practitioners of a brand of white identity politics?

But other parts of Fukuyama's argument are more persuasive, and he is right to focus on the role that identity plays in the health of American democracy. Fukuyama makes one particularly useful point in the closing passages of his article:

> People will never stop thinking about themselves and their societies in identity terms. But people's identities are neither fixed nor necessarily given by birth. Identity can be used to divide, but it can also be used to unify. That, in the end, will be the remedy for the populist politics of the present.

What Fukuyama gets right here is the fact that human beings have a fundamental need to belong—a need that their collective identities, be they racial, ethnic, religious, regional, or national, often satisfy. Such affiliations, which psychologists call "social identities," serve multiple psychological functions. These include, for example, the need for a sense of safety, which social identities satisfy by reducing uncertainty and providing norms that help people navigate everyday life. Some social identities also offer rituals and customs to aid with loss, mourning, and other significant challenges that occur during the course of one's life. At times, identities provide a sense of purpose and meaning and a basis for esteem and regard that is larger than people's individual selves. As Fukuyama suggests, identities efficiently satisfy the human need for respect and dignity.

What Fukuyama gets wrong, however, is the idea that a single unifying identity—a "creedal" American identity—could alone satisfy this suite of psychological needs and thereby allow citizens to abandon the smaller social identities

What makes it different is how tightly Americans' views about racial, ethnic, and religious identities are now bound up with another salient American identity: partisan affiliation.

that people invest in and clearly value. Broad identities such as the one Fukuyama promotes are useful and unifying at times, but they rarely meet the human need for individuation. That is why people look to narrower bases for identification. Moreover, broad social identities such as national affiliations—even when ostensibly based on principles that are hypothetically accessible to all—often rely on the terms and norms of the dominant majority and thus end up undermining the identity needs of minority groups.

Furthermore, people's existing social identities are important to them, and attempts to dissolve them would likely be met with severe resistance. The potential loss of a group's identity, real or imagined, is psychologically threatening. A powerful urge compels people to defend their groups at all costs in the face of such threats. As Fukuyama himself notes, a sense of loss due to the changing racial and ethnic composition of the United States is partly to blame for the rise of right-wing identity politics. Hence, it is important not only to cultivate a common American identity, as Fukuyama argues, but also to promote the idea of the United States as inclusive of multiple racial, ethnic, religious, and other types of identities. Indeed, Americans must create that society.

Why Don't We Have Both?

Perhaps the main weakness of Fukuyama's argument is the implication that Americans face a binary choice when it comes to political identity: either they can embrace a broad creedal identity or they can cling to narrow identities based on race, ethnicity, gender, or ideology. There is no reason to think that is true. Political leaders can address the sense of psychological vulnerability triggered by shifting demographics and social change and also respect rightful claims for inclusion and fair treatment on the part of members of marginalized groups. Americans can acknowledge and, when appropriate, celebrate the particular identities, cultures, and histories of distinct social groups and also pursue a unifying national creed.

There is even some evidence to suggest that the more identities people maintain—and the more complex and overlapping those identities are—the less conflict they will have with people who maintain different sets of identities. Greater identity complexity may serve as a buffer against the feelings of humiliation and resentment that often fuel ethnonationalist movements.

Identifying as American does not require the relinquishing of other identities. In fact, it is possible to leverage those identities to cultivate and deepen one's Americanness. For instance, researchers have found that when people highlight their shared experiences, even when they belong to what appear to be opposing, if not adversarial, social groups, they experience an increase in empathy and harmony. Rather than dividing people, the act of reflecting on the marginalization of one's own social group—be it current or historical—can encourage societal cohesion.

In the United States, an honest accounting and acknowledgment of what it has meant to be American could reveal Americans' shared vulnerability and their common capacity for wrongdoing, as well as their resilience in the face of mistreatment. This sentiment is echoed by the lawyer and civil rights activist Bryan Stevenson, who has argued for the need to engage honestly with the history of racial injustice in the United States. "We can create communities in this country where people are less burdened by our history of racial inequality," Stevenson told an interviewer last year. "The more we understand the depth of that suffering, the more we understand the power of people to cope and overcome and survive."

That sounds like a unifying national creed that would allow Americans to embrace their own identities, encourage them to respect the identities embraced by others, and affirm shared principles of equality and justice. Fukuyama appears to believe that this more complex form of national identification is not possible. I think it is. It may even be the only path toward a diverse nation that lives up to its democratic principles.

Jennifer A. Richeson is Philip R. Allen Professor of Psychology at Yale University.

FUKUYAMA REPLIES

I appreciate these thoughtful comments on my article. But all three responses, which contain a number of common themes, fundamentally miscast my thinking about identity politics. One reason for this might be that the article focuses more on the kind of identity politics characteristic of the contemporary progressive left, whereas the book from which the article was adapted, *Identity*, focuses more on my central concern: the recent rise of right-wing nationalist populism. This development threatens liberal democracy because populist leaders seek to use the legitimacy they gain from democratic elections to undermine liberal institutions such as courts, the media, and impartial bureaucracies. This has been happening in Hungary, Poland, and, above all, the United States. Populists' distrust of "globalism" also leads them to weaken the international institutions necessary to manage the liberal world order.

I concur with the commonplace judgment that the rise of populism has been triggered by globalization and the consequent massive increase in inequality in many rich countries. But if the fundamental cause were merely economic, one would have expected to see left-wing populism everywhere; instead, since the 2008 financial crisis, parties on the left have been in decline, while the most energized new movements have been anti-immigrant groups, such as the far-right party Alternative for Germany and the populist coalition now governing Italy. In the 2016 U.S. presidential election, enough white working-class voters abandoned the Democratic Party to put Donald Trump over the top, capping a 40-year trend of shifting party loyalties. This means that there is something going on in the cultural realm that needs explaining, and that something is concern over identity.

Balancing Identity

The concept of "identity," as I use the term, builds on a universal aspect of the human psyche that Plato labeled *thymos*, the demand for respect for one's inner dignity. But there is a specifically modern expression of *thymos* that emerged after the Protestant Reformation and that values the inner self more highly than society's laws, norms, and customs and insists that society change its own norms to give recognition to that inner self. The first major expression of modern identity politics was nineteenth-century European nationalism, when cultural groups began to demand recognition in the form of statehood. I believe that much of modern Islamism is similarly driven by identity confusion among Muslims in modernizing societies who feel neither Western nor traditional and see a particular form of politicized religion as a source of community and identity.

But it is not correct to say, as John Sides, Michael Tesler, Lynn Vavreck, and Jennifer Richeson do, that identity politics as I define it drove white-supremacist and anti-immigrant movements in the nineteenth-century United States. Racism and xenophobia have always existed. But a generation or two ago, white Americans did not typically think of themselves as a victimized minority mistreated by elites who were indifferent to their problems. Today, many do, because contemporary racists have borrowed their framing of identity from groups on the left, in ways that resonate with people who are not necessarily racist.

Another major misunderstanding of my argument has to do with my view of contemporary identity movements such as Black Lives Matter and #MeToo. Of course they are rooted in real social injustices such as police violence and sexual harassment; they legitimately call for concrete policy remedies and a broad shift in cultural norms. But people can walk and chew gum at the same time. Even as Americans seek to right injustices suffered by specific social groups, they need to balance their small-group identities with a more integrative identity needed to create a cohesive national democratic community. I am not arguing, contrary to Richeson, that this will be an adequate substitute for narrower identities; rather, it will be a complement to them.

Liberal democracy cannot exist without a national identity that defines what citizens hold in common with one another. Given the de facto multiculturalism of contemporary democracies, that identity needs to be civic or creedal. That is, it needs to be based on liberal political ideas that are accessible to people of different cultural backgrounds rather than on fixed characteristics such as race, ethnicity, or religion. I thought that the United States had arrived at such a creedal identity in the wake of the civil rights movement, but that accomplishment is now being threatened by right-wing identitarians, led by Trump, who would like to drag Americans backward to identities based on ethnicity and religion.

Winning vs. Governing

Stacey Abrams criticizes my desire to return to class as the defining target of progressive politics, since class and race overlap strongly in the United States. But it is absurd to see white Americans as a uniformly privileged category, as she seems to do. A significant part of the white working class has followed the black working class into underclass status. Communities facing deindustrialization and job loss have experienced increases in crime, family breakdown, and drug use; the Centers for Disease Control and Prevention has estimated that 72,000 Americans died in 2017 of drug overdoses related to the opioid epidemic. So although part of the populist vote both in the United States and in Europe is driven by racism and xenophobia, part of it is driven by legitimate complaints that elites—the mainstream political parties, the media, cultural institutions, and major corporations—have failed to recognize these voters' plight and have stood by as this decline has occurred.

Abrams knows much better than I do what is required to win an election in the contemporary United States, and I'm sorry that she did not succeed in her bid for governor of Georgia. But I'm not sure that a successful electoral strategy would necessarily translate into a sustainable governing strategy. The country's single greatest weakness today is the intense polarization that has infected its political system, a weakness that has been exploited by authoritarian rivals such as China and Russia. In practical terms, overcoming polarization means devising a posture that will win back at least part of the white working-class vote that has shifted from the left to the right. Peeling away populist voters not driven by simple racism means taking seriously some of their concerns over cultural change and national identity. I agree that the burden is on Republican politicians to stop defending Trump, but they will do so only when they realize that their own voters are turning against him.

The contemporary Middle East, like the Balkans before it, is an extreme example of out-of-control identity politics and what ultimately happens to countries that do not invest in integrative national identities. The United States is fortunately far from that point of state breakdown. But what is happening in the country is part of a larger global shift from a politics based on economic ideas to a politics based on identity. In the 2018 midterm elections, Trump was reportedly advised by Paul Ryan, the Republican Speaker of the House, to campaign on the 2017 tax cut and economic growth; Trump chose instead to go the identity route by railing against migrant caravans and birthright citizenship. This is identity politics on steroids.

This shift, echoed in other countries, is not compatible with modern liberal democracy. The latter is rooted in the rights of individuals, and not the rights of groups or fixed communities. And unless the United States counters this trend domestically, it will continue to set a bad example for the rest of the world.

Print Citations

CMS: Abrams, Stacey Y., Sides, John, Tesler, Michael, Vavreck, Lynn, Richeson, Jennifer A., and Francis Fukuyama. "E Pluribus Unum? The Fight Over Identity Politics." In *The Reference Shelf: Democracy Evolving,* edited by Micah L. Issitt, 62-73. Amenia, NY: Grey House Publishing, 2019.

MLA: Abrams, Stacey Y., Sides, John, Tesler, Michael, Vavreck, Lynn, Richeson, Jennifer A., and Francis Fukuyama. "E Pluribus Unum? The Fight Over Identity Politics." *The Reference Shelf Democracy Evolving,* edited by Micah L. Issitt, Grey Housing Publishing, 2019, pp. 62-73.

APA: Abrams, S.Y., Sides J., Tesler, M., Vavreck, L., Richeson, J.A., & Fukuyama, F. (2019). E pluribus unum? The fight over identity politics. In Micah L. Issitt (Ed.), *The reference shelf: Democracy evolving* (pp. 62-73). Amenia, NY: Grey Housing Publishing.

3
Democracy or Dictatorship?

Although the concentration of power in the executive branch was not begun by Donald Trump, his frequent attempts to bypass traditional checks and balances have led to many protests against his authoritarian tendencies.

Democratic Authoritarianism

Authoritarianism can be defined as a form of government based on arbitrary authority and in which the state utilizes the law to prohibit resistance to state policies. Authoritarian governments are becoming more prominent in the twenty-first century, driven by a resurgence of right-wing conservatism in Europe and North America. In the United States, critics have accused President Trump of either being authoritarian or of supporting an authoritarian view of America's future, accusations related to Trump administration attempts to reinterpret executive authority so as to grant Trump greater power to enact policy changes without congressional oversight. Trump has also led an attack against the legitimacy of the mainstream press, a pattern common in authoritarian governments and one that threatens the integrity of any democratic society by leading the people away from legitimate sources of information that empower their participation in government.[1]

Authoritarianism and Conservatism

In the United States, there is an increasing tendency for citizens to view the political world through a bifurcated lens that they may conceptualize as conservative and liberal, or right-wing and left-wing. Currently, the rise in authoritarianism around the world is being driven by radical conservatism, and this creates the false impression that conservatism is inherently authoritarian. In reality, those who identify as either liberal or conservative can both embrace authoritarianism in certain situations.[2] Whether individuals tend toward authoritarianism depends on the nature of the political threats that members of a certain group perceive, and on which individuals or groups they have identified as enemies or outsiders. The tendency to embrace authoritarianism is situational and is related to which perceived group dominates the social and political environment.[3]

On a more philosophical level, psychologists and social scientists sometimes refer to what is known as "authoritarian" thought, which can be described as psychological tendencies that make it more likely for a person to embrace authoritarian policies. One is a tendency to develop views on certain topics based on the views of someone in authority whom the individual holds in high regard, rather than based on the information or data that might be available on an issue. Individuals who embrace highly fundamentalist views on religion typically display this tendency, developing world views based on the authority of religious scriptures or certain religious teachers alone. At different points in American history, there has been a synthesis of conservatism and authoritarianism, typically occurring at times when a certain proportion of conservatives have come to believe that more extreme measures are needed to protect their culture or values. For example, conservative support for the anti-communism movement of the 1940s and ʼ50s, with the perceived threat of communist subversion, caused American conservatives to favor policies that violated constitutional protections on individual liberty. Similarly, many American conservatives have been willing to accept authoritarian philosophy with regard to America's policies on Muslim immigrants, citizens, and refugees, based on the sense that the threat of Islamic terrorism warrants policies that might otherwise be seen as violating constitutional protections regarding due process, civil liberty, and individual freedom.

The modern shift toward authoritarianism in the twenty-first century has been driven by right-wing ideology, and this reflects the evolution of global popular culture over the past half century. A confluence of factors has gradually led to a liberalization of popular culture on the global scale, a pattern made more prevalent by the increasing global connectivity of the digital age. This has resulted in a push for inclusivity in education, government, and in society in general, eroding the status and popular influence of conservatives in many societies. Viewing the emerging norms of popular culture as increasingly hostile, individuals with right-wing political and social views have gravitated toward radicalism. In the United States, the increasing visibility of the "alt-right," a digital-age version of American white nationalism, is an example of this trend. The racial and gender-role status quo favored by members of the alt-right was once mainstream, but has increasingly become a fringe in American culture. Thus, alt-right activists have become more radical. Likewise, Islamic radicals represent a conservative, fundamentalist view of society that was once the status quo across much of the world. As this highly religious version of global culture has begun to wane in influence, adherents have gathered into militant groups in an attempt to violently reinstate the previous status quo, which included a strict hierarchy of power involving gender and racial groups.

Centralization of American Power

The U.S. government was designed to prohibit tyranny and to prevent America from slipping into dictatorship or authoritarianism. Key to maintaining this balance are laws that prohibit individuals in any branch of government from exerting unchecked power. Congress was intended to be the most powerful of the branches of government because it most directly reflects the popular will and is composed of individuals elected directly to represent specific populations. Political analysts have argued that the Trump administration has participated in an attempt to consolidate executive power, which some call authoritarian.[4]

The perception that Trump's approach to the presidency is authoritarian or dictatorial is largely a matter of perspective. There have been many instances when past presidents have arguably exceeded their constitutionally mandated powers. The internment of Japanese Americans by Franklin Roosevelt is one example. Abraham Lincoln's emancipation proclamation ending slavery is another. Barack Obama's administration used an executive order as a temporary measure to establish the DACA program for children of immigrants born in the United States. Some argue that the expansion of the powers in the executive branch began with Theodore Roosevelt's conservation campaign. Roosevelt wrote in his 1913 biography: "I did not usurp power, but I did greatly broaden the use of executive power."[5] Whether or not such actions are embraced by the public depends on the public's perception of the need for such actions. Trump promotes his use of executive authority as necessary based on what he depicts as a conspiracy against him led by an alliance of liberal politicians. Trump supporters have demonstrated a tendency to view his use of executive authority as appropriate while decrying as illegal or unconstitutional the same use of executive authority by a president with whom they disagree. Citizens support broad use of presidential authority when it supports their own views, and criticize similar employment of executive authority when it establishes policies with which they disagree.

It might be argued that several presidents violated constitutional principles by failing to appropriately delegate or relinquish authority to Congress. There is no clear precedent concerning presidential authority; powers ascribed to the presidency are the least clearly defined of any of the three branches, and the debate over presidential authority is only made more complicated by partisanship.[6]

Political activists, members of the public, and political scientists have suggested that President Trump is pushing America toward authoritarianism, a perception is shaped, in part, by his tendency to voice authoritarian ideas in his public statements. For example, Trump suggested that members of Congress who refused to applaud his achievements during his State of the Union speech might be guilty of treason. Suggesting that it might be criminal to oppose or criticize a sitting president keeps with the strategies of authoritarian dictators, used to foster the belief that questioning authority is unpatriotic, a belief that is clearly anathema to the ideals of American democracy. Questioning presidential, congressional, and all other forms of authority has been a fundamental characteristic of American society since framers of the constitution endeavored to free America from the yoke of authoritarian rule under the crown of Britain. Regardless of the sincerity of Trump's statement, it fueled the perception that Trump has authoritarian tendencies.

Though opinions on this issue are highly divided, it's possible that Trump supporters may develop false ideas about concepts like treason, which could be detrimental not only to appropriately enforcing federal law, but to the health of our democracy. When any large percentage of Americans feel that there is a problem with America's government, this problem is legitimate, even if other Americans disagree.

Works Used

Boissoneault, Lorraine. "The Debate over Executive Orders Began with Teddy Roosevelt's Mad Passion for Conservation." *Smithsonian.com*. Retrieved from https://www.smithsonianmag.com/history/how-theodore-roosevelts-executive-orders-reshaped-countryand-presidency-180962908/.

Bump, Philip. "The President Was Never Intended to Be the Most Powerful Part of Government." *The Washington Post*. Feb 13, 2017. Retrieved from   https://www.washingtonpost.com/news/politics/wp/2017/02/13/

the-president-was-never-intended-to-be-the-most-powerful-part-of-government/?noredirect=on&utm_term=.2b1f5f74e44e.

Chait, Jonathan. "Conservatives Can't Distinguish Between Democratic Reform and Authoritarianism." *New York*. Mar 29, 2019. Retrieved from http://nymag.com/intelligencer/2019/03/trump-authoritarian-electoral-college-popular-vote-democracy.html.

Crowson, H.M, Thoma, S.J., and Hestevold, N. "Is Political Conservatism Synonymous with Authoritarianism? *Journal of Social Psychology*. 2005. Oct, Vol. 145, No. 5, 571-92.

Gonzales, Richard. "5 Questions About DACA Answered." *NPR*. Sep 5, 2017. Retrieved from https://www.npr.org/2017/09/05/548754723/5-things-you-should-know-about-daca.

Jacobson, Louis. "Donald Trump's Pants on Fire Claim about 'Treason'." *Politifact*. Feb 6, 2018. Retrieved from https://www.politifact.com/truth-o-meter/statements/2018/feb/06/donald-trump/donald-trumps-pants-fire-claim-about-treason/.

Singal, Jesse. "How Social Science Might Be Misunderstanding Conservatives." *New York*. Jul 15, 2018. Retrieved from http://nymag.com/intelligencer/2018/07/how-social-science-might-be-misunderstanding-conservatives.html.

Stephan, Maria J. and Timothy Snyder. "Authoritarianism Is Making a Comeback: Here's the Time-Tested Way to Defeat It." *The Guardian*. Jun 20, 2017. Retrieved from https://www.theguardian.com/commentisfree/2017/jun/20/authoritarianism-trump-resistance-defeat.

Suedfeld, Peter. "Authoritarian Thinking, Groupthink, and Decision-Making Under Stress: Are Simple Decisions Always Worse?" *American Psychological Association*. August 1986.

"Theodore Roosevelt." Retrieved from https://www.whitehouse.gov/about-the-white-house/presidents/theodore-roosevelt/.

Notes

1. Stephan and Snyder, "Authoritarianism Is Making a Comeback: Here's the Time-Tested Way to Defeat It."
2. Crowson, Thoma, and Hestevold, "Is Political Conservatism Synonymous with Authoritarianism?"
3. Singal, "How Social Science Might Be Misunderstanding Conservatives."
4. Bump, "The President Was Never Intended to Be the Most Powerful Part of Government."
5. "Theodore Roosevelt."; Boissoneault, Lorraine. "The Debate over Executive Orders Began with Teddy Roosevelt's Mad Passion for Conservation."
6. Chait, "Conservatives Can't Distinguish Between Democratic Reform and Authoritarianism."

American Democracy Is in Crisis, and Not Just Because of Trump

By Simon Tisdall

The Guardian, **August 7, 2018**

Nineteen months into the Trump presidency, US democracy is running into serious trouble—but it is not all, or even mostly, Donald Trump's fault. This crisis of governance has been building for decades. It is only now, as Trump's iconoclastic assaults on established beliefs, laws, institutions and values test the system to destruction, that the true scale of pre-existing weaknesses and faultlines is becoming apparent.

This deep crisis of confidence, bordering on national meltdown, comes as the US hurtles towards midterm elections in November—a familiar American ritual now rendered strangely unpredictable by fears of foreign manipulation and an FBI investigation that could, by some estimates, lead ultimately to Trump's impeachment. The process of degradation affects US citizens and all those around the world who hold up the US democratic system as a paradigm worthy of emulation. Friends worry that the country's ability to sustain its traditional global leadership role—moral and practical—is being undermined. Enemies, principally anti-democratic, authoritarian competitor regimes in Russia and China, hope this is so.

Take a case in point, with global implications: Trump has repeatedly bragged about his willingness to use nuclear weapons. As commander-in-chief, he oversees the world's largest nuclear arsenal. Last year he threatened to "totally destroy" North Korea, a nation of 25 million people. He has also threatened Iran. Such lunatic recklessness appalls many Americans. But it transpires there is little they could do to stop Trump should he decide, on a whim, to press the "nuclear button".

Checks do exist. There is a chain of command that cannot be bypassed. But security experts say nobody, not even the secretaries of state and defence or the chairman of the joint chiefs, has legal power to block a presidential launch order. What could be less democratic? Yet this dilemma was not created by Trump. It has existed for many years. Congress is now belatedly reviewing it.

Trump's frequent use of "executive orders" has provided another wake-up call. Most infamous was his travel ban on people from seven Muslim-majority countries, but others—concerning his Mexican border wall, his unilateral imposition of steel tariffs, and his reversal of Barack Obama's Affordable Care Act—were also highly contentious. Yet, once issued, such orders are rarely overturned. After numerous legal challenges, the supreme court upheld the travel ban.

Many were shocked to discover that a US president could issue diktats and fat-was like the worst kind of unelected despot or ayatollah. But the use of such orders, avoiding public scrutiny, is long-established. Franklin Roosevelt interned Japanese-Americans after Pearl Harbor by this means. Abraham Lincoln's emancipation proclamation ending slavery was an executive order. In exercising this arbitrary power, Trump is following precedent, however undemocratic. The expanding powers of what the Vietnam-era historian Arthur Schlesinger dubbed the "imperial presidency" is a long-recognised phenomenon and one that Congress, America's primary constitutional pillar, has signally failed to curb over the years. This may be one reason why Americans, according to polling going back decades, exhibit a consistently low opinion of Congress. But there are many others. The dominant two-party system, virulent partisanship and out-of-touch politicians are blamed for chronic failures of governance. The advantages conferred by incumbency are overwhelming; most members are repeatedly re-elected, reducing democratic choice. In terms of the presidency—the second constitutional pillar—systemic problems produce even greater anomalies. Trump was the fifth president to win office despite losing the popular vote, thanks to the archaic, unaccountably unreformed electoral college process.

Members of Congress are widely viewed as overly beholden to corporations, wealthy donors and special interests. In other words, they are seen as corrupt. The sums involved in greasing the wheels of US democracy are indeed eye-watering. According to the campaign finance watchdog Open Secrets, an overall $6.5bn (£5bn) was spent by presidential and congressional

> **Decades of complacent assumptions about America's unending, unquestioning adherence to the democratic model have left it vulnerable to subversion within and without.**

candidates in 2016—enough to give every teacher in the country a $2,000 pay rise.

The average cost of winning a Senate seat was $19.4m. Winning a House of Representatives seat in the midterm elections will cost an average $1.5m, at least. The need for such huge war chests effectively excludes many would-be candidates from the democratic process and places others in hock to their financial backers.

Again, worries over excessive, non-transparent or illegal campaign financing long precede Trump. Despite many reform efforts, a growing proportion of funding comes from anonymous sources. According to a recent USA Today investigation, 40% of all television ads for political candidates are financed by secret donors with private political or commercial agendas. Then there is untraceable money emanating from foreign governments or individuals, via agents and lobbyists—an issue of heightened concern in the context of the Mueller inquiry into Trump's 2016 campaign.

Mounting evidence of Russian influence-peddling and meddling has added to the sense of a gathering crisis of democracy. Yet while Trump's minimising of the issue and his attempts to shut down the Mueller probe are plainly self-interested, these problems cannot all be laid at his door. Russians have been seeking to undermine US democracy since 1945. The difference now is they're getting better at it —as are other foreign states.

US intelligence chiefs agree. "Our democracy itself is in the crosshairs," the homeland security secretary, Kirstjen Nielsen, said last week. "Free and fair elections are the cornerstone of our democracy, and it has become clear that they are the target of our adversaries, who seek … to sow discord and undermine our way of life." Yet what if Trump really were to be proven guilty of conspiring with a foreign power? How would he react? This is unknown, scary territory.

Can the judicial branch and, in particular, the supreme court—the third constitutional pillar and proud symbol of the founding fathers' doctrine of the separation of powers—save US democracy? It seems unlikely. In nominating a prominent conservative, Brett Kavanaugh, for the latest court vacancy, Trump followed recent practice in shaping the court to suit his political outlook. It has not always worked this way. As the author David Greenberg has pointed out, supreme court nominations used to be mostly apolitical. This is not the constitution envisaged when they wrote the rules in Philadelphia in 1787.

Rudy Giuliani Has Turned Out to Be a Dangerous Liability for Trump

Trump's maverick behaviour highlights these entrenched structural problems. Yet, that aside, his rogue presidency is uniquely corrosive, right now, of democracy everywhere. His encouragement of ultranationalist, racist and neo-fascist forces from Warsaw to Charlottesville, divisive demagoguery, relentless vilification of independent journalism, contempt for the western European democracies, coddling of dictators and rejection of the established, rules-based international order all reinforce perceptions that the global role of the US as shining democratic beacon is dimming rapidly. Trump did this all by himself.

So what is to be done? The most urgent task is to recognise what is happening. Decades of complacent assumptions about America's unending, unquestioning adherence to the democratic model have left it vulnerable to subversion within and without. Radical, inclusive political reform is urgently required. There needs to be a national conversation—and a revisiting of basic democratic principles. Maybe it's time, 231 years on, for a follow-up constitutional convention in Philadelphia?

Print Citations

CMS: Tisdall, Simon. "American Democracy Is in Crisis, and Not Just Because of Trump." In *The Reference Shelf: Democracy Evolving*, edited by Micah L. Issitt, 81-84. Amenia, NY: Grey House Publishing, 2019.

MLA: Tisdall, Simon. "American Democracy Is in Crisis, and Not Just Because of Trump." *The Reference Shelf: Democracy Evolving*, edited by Micah L. Issitt, Grey Housing Publishing, 2019, pp. 81-84.

APA: Tisdall, S. (2019). American democracy is in crisis, and not just because of Trump. In Micah L. Issitt (Ed.), *The reference shelf: Democracy evolving* (pp. 81-84). Amenia, NY: Grey Housing Publishing.

American Democracy Has Gone Through Dark Times Before

Robert Dallek

The Guardian, November 1, 2017

The announcements that Paul Manafort, Rick Gates and George Papadopoulos have been indicted by a federal grand jury on various charges, including conspiring against the United States, money laundering and lying to the Federal Bureau of Investigation (FBI) deepens the current cynicism about politics, politicians and the Trump administration in particular.

According to the *Washington Post*, seven out of 10 Americans see the country being as sharply divided into warring political camps as during the Vietnam war 50 years ago. The division and inability of the Trump administration to pass any major legislative initiative about immigration, healthcare and now possibly federal taxes, despite Trump's repeated promises about making America great again, create doubts about democracy's effectiveness as a system of government.

Current events remind some people of Winston Churchill's famous observation that democracy is the worst possible system—except for all the rest. Or maybe it's just like all the rest. What makes it particularly distressing is the view that this is not an aberration but rather the "new normal".

It might help Americans to remember that we have been through these periods of disillusionment before.

In the 19th century, the country was torn apart by the civil war. More than 600,000 residents of the north and south perished in the fighting (and this in the era before machine guns, lethal long-range artillery, aircraft and atom bombs that killed tens of millions in the two world wars). At the time, Americans struggled to believe that the United States could ever function again as a unified nation.

In the 1920s and 1930s, the durability of democracy once again seemed doubtful. The split between rural fundamentalists and urban modernists, between recent migrants to the United States from eastern and southern Europe and older assimilated Americans found expression in the National Origins Act of 1924, a discriminatory immigration act.

The so-called Scopes monkey trial in 1925 over the teaching of evolution in high school biology classes, which pitted religious reformists and secularists against fundamentalists, and the famous Sacco-Vanzetti murder case, which saw two Italian-American anarchists executed in a highly contentious case, convinced Americans

> **It might help Americans to remember that we have been through these periods of disillusionment before.**

that the country was permanently divided.

The country found momentary relief in the 1928 election of Herbert Hoover, who seemed to promise a new era of prosperity that would dissolve social tensions. But the onset of the Great Depression, with the stock market crash in 1929 and the downward spiral of the economy in 1930-1932, stimulated renewed fears that free enterprise and democracy in America were over. Hoover lamented the absence of a joke, a song or a story that could lift the pall of pessimism that had descended on the country.

The election of Franklin D Roosevelt in 1932 proved to be the palliative that gave people hope. His fireside chats and many legislative initiatives not only lifted the spirits of the country, but also humanized the American industrial system and brought the country into the 20th century.

His introduction of the Federal Emergency Relief Administration; the Tennessee Valley Authority, the Securities and Exchange Commission, the Civilian Conservation Corps, the Federal Deposit Insurance Corporation, the National Youth Administration, social security, the Public Works Administration, the Works Progress Administration, the wages and hours law, setting minimum wages and maximum hours and the dam-building that promoted conservation and economic expansion all helped achieve this turnaround.

FDR's determination to bring representatives of recent immigrant groups—Catholics and Jews, southern and eastern Europeans of every stripe—into the mainstream of the country's life, while attending to the needs of white rural southerners, largely healed the divide of the 1920s.

He was much less attentive to the abuse of African Americans by racists guilty of lynching. But the benefits to black Americans from the New Deal alphabet agencies shifted the loyalty of black voters from the Republicans to the Democrats. It was all a prelude to the unity of the country that marked its response to Pearl Harbor and the struggle to win the second world war.

The struggle to maintain national unity dissolved again in the Cold War, with conservative complaints that Democrats had fallen short in defending the country's national security against communist advances across Europe and Asia.

Accusations about Roosevelt's appeasement of Stalin at the Yalta Conference in February 1945 and Harry Truman's failure to save China from Mao Zedong's communist takeover, underscored by Senator Joseph McCarthy's charges of subversion by US government officials and anger over the stalemate in the Korean war once again demoralized the country. It was a prelude to the bitter struggle over the failure in Vietnam.

The tensions now over Donald Trump's alleged collaboration with the Kremlin to assure his victory in the 2016 election and the charges of administration corruption echo the run-up to Richard Nixon's Watergate scandal.

We of course don't know where the current divide will end. While it certainly looks like another moment in the repeated history of America's domestic struggles, it is a familiar enough battle to reassure downcast citizens that we have a resilient democracy that will generate another period of national cooperation and advance. Or at least, we can hope so!

Print Citations

CMS: Dallek, Robert. "American Democracy Has Gone Through Dark Times Before." In *The Reference Shelf: Democracy Evolving*, edited by Micah L. Issitt, 85-87. Amenia, NY: Grey House Publishing, 2019.

MLA: Dallek, Robert. "American Democracy Has Gone Through Dark Times Before." *The Reference Shelf: Democracy Evolving*, edited by Micah L. Issitt, Grey Housing Publishing, 2019, pp. 85-87.

APA: Dallek, R. (2019). American democracy has gone through dark times before. In Micah L. Issitt (Ed.), *The reference shelf: Democracy evolving* (pp. 85-87). Amenia, NY: Grey Housing Publishing.

Lessons in the Decline of Democracy from the Ruined Roman Republic

By Jason Daley

Smithsonian Magazine, November 6, 2018

The U.S. Constitution owes a huge debt to ancient Rome. The Founding Fathers were well-versed in Greek and Roman History. Leaders like Thomas Jefferson and James Madison read the historian Polybius, who laid out one of the clearest descriptions of the Roman Republic's constitution, where representatives of various factions and social classes checked the power of the elites and the power of the mob. It's not surprising that in the United States' nascent years, comparisons to ancient Rome were common. And to this day, Rome, whose 482-year-long Republic, bookended by several hundred years of monarchy and 1,500 years of imperial rule, is still the longest the world has seen.

Aspects of our modern politics reminded University of California San Diego historian Edward Watts of the last century of the Roman Republic, roughly 130 B.C. to 27 B.C. That's why he took a fresh look at the period in his new book *Mortal Republic: How Rome Fell Into Tyranny*. Watts chronicles the ways the republic, with a population once devoted to national service and personal honor, was torn to shreds by growing wealth inequality, partisan gridlock, political violence and pandering politicians, and argues that the people of Rome chose to let their democracy die by not protecting their political institutions, eventually turning to the perceived stability of an emperor instead of facing the continued violence of an unstable and degraded republic. Political messaging during the 2018 midterm elections hinged on many of these exact topics.

Though he does not directly compare and contrast Rome with the United States, Watts says that what took place in Rome is a lesson for all modern republics. "Above all else, the Roman Republic teaches the citizens of its modern descendants the incredible dangers that come along with condoning political obstruction and courting political violence," he writes. "Roman history could not more clearly show that, when citizens look away as their leaders engage in these corrosive behaviors, their republic is in mortal danger."

Historians are cautious when trying to apply lessons from one unique culture to another, and the differences between the modern United States and Rome are immense. Rome was an Iron-Age city-state with a government-sponsored religion that at times made decisions by looking at the entrails of sheep. Romans had a rigid class system, relied on slave labor and had a tolerance for everyday violence that is genuinely horrifying. Then again, other aspects of the Roman Republic feel rather familiar.

The Roman people's strong sense of patriotism was unique in the Mediterranean world. Like the United States after World War II, Rome, after winning the Second Punic War in 201 B.C. (the one with Hannibal and the elephants), became the world's hegemon, which lead to a massive increase in their military spending, a baby boom, and gave rise to a class of super-wealthy elites that were able to use their money to influence politics and push their own agendas. Those similarities make comparisons worthwhile, even if the togas, gladiator battles and appetite for dormice seem completely foreign.

Cullen Murphy, whose 2005 book *Are We Rome?* makes a more head-on comparison between the fall of the Roman Empire and the U.S., argues that the changes in politics and society in Rome stemmed from one source: its growing complexity. Rome, during the Republic and Empire, had increasing and evolving responsibilities around the Mediterranean which its government constantly struggled to manage. Those challenges forced changes throughout the economy and society, sometimes for the better and sometimes for the worse. In general terms, he sees many of the same struggles in recent U.S. history.

"I think the U.S. is experiencing this same situation—we've never quite recovered from our victory in World War II, which left us with the world on our shoulders; and the implications of that responsibility have skewed things in every part of our society and economy, and put our old political (and other) structures under enormous strain," he says. "New sources of power and new forms of administration and management fill the gap—and create unease and sometimes also injustice, and at the same time create vast new sectors of wealth."

Those types of social and economic changes also rattled the Roman Republic, leading to the moment in 130 B.C. when politics turned violent. The introduction of a secret ballot meant Roman politicians and political factions couldn't keep tabs on (or bribe) individual voters. Instead, politicians had to build political brands that appealed to the masses, leading to something akin to modern American campaigning with big promises and populist language aimed at the poor and middle class.

Reforms to the military also meant that service was no longer reserved for the elite, who for centuries used their privilege to demonstrate their loyalty to Rome. For poorer soldiers, however, service became a path to riches. They began to count on the loot, bonuses and gifts of land they received from their often-wealthy commanders meaning that over time the loyalty of the Roman legions shifted from the empire to their generals. These changes set the stage for a new type of politics, one where whipping up the resentments of the lower classes and threatening political enemies with semi-private armies became the norm.

These trends first came to a head in 134 B.C. when Tiberius Gracchus, an elected tribune of the people, proposed a land reform bill that would benefit poorer and middle-class Romans. The way Gracchus went about his reform, however, was an affront to the norms and traditions of the Republic. He brought his law before the

Plebeian Assembly without the thumbs-up of the Senate. When his fellow tribune Marcus Octavius threatened to veto the bill, which was his right, Gracchus manipulated the rules to have him stripped of his office. There were other incidents as well, but the most concerning aspect of Gracchus was his fiery, populist language, which whipped his supporters to the edge of political violence. As his power grew, Gracchus began moving through the streets surrounded by a mob of frenzied supporters, a kind of personal militia not seen in Rome before.

Rumors spread that Gracchus was angling to become a king or dictator, and some in the Senate felt they needed to act. When Gracchus stood for a second term as tribune, which was not illegal but broke another norm, a group of Senators and their supporters beat Gracchus and 300 of his followers to death.

It was just the beginning. Over the next century, Tiberius's brother Gaius Gracchus would come into conflict with the Senate after a similar populist confrontation. The commander Sulla would march legions loyal to him on Rome itself and battle his political rival Marius, the first time Roman troops fought one another. He would then execute and punish his political enemies. In the following generation Pompey and Caesar would settle their political scores using

> **We do need to assign blame to politicians and individuals who take a shortsighted view of the health of a republic in order to try to pursue their own personal objectives or specific short-term political advantages.**

Roman legions, Octavian and Marc Antony would field an army against the Senate before finally battling one another bringing almost 500 years of the Republic to a bloody (and confusing) conclusion.

Watts argues that while the Senate ordered his murder, it was Tiberius Gracchus who let the genie out of the bottle. "What he has to bear responsibility for is he starts using this really aggressive and threatening language and threatening postures. He never resorts to violence, but there's always this implicit threat. 'If not for me, things would get out of control.' And that is different, that was never done before. What he introduces is this political tool of intimidation and threats of violence. Later thinkers say once it's there, even if others choose not to use it, it's there forever."

While life in Rome, with gladiator battles, crucifixions and endless war was violent, for centuries Romans took pride in their republican system and political violence was taboo. "The Republic was free of political violence for the better part of 300 years. People who are politically engaged are not killing each other and they're not threatening to kill each other. When they disagree with each other they use political means that were created by the republic for dealing with political conflict," says Watts. "If you lose one of those conflicts, you don't die and you don't lose your property and you aren't sent away. You just lose face and move on. In that sense, this is a remarkably successful system for encouraging compromise and encouraging consensus building and creating mechanisms whereby political conflicts will be decided peacefully."

So what does the story of the Roman Republic mean for the United States? The comparison is not perfect. The U.S. has had its share of political violence over the centuries and has more or less recovered. Politicians used to regularly duel one another (See the *Hamilton* soundtrack, song 15), and in the run-up to the Civil War, the ultimate act of political violence, there was the raid on Harper's Ferry, Bleeding Kansas, and the near murder of Charles Sumner in the Senate chamber. Joanne B. Freeman, author of *Field of Blood*, a history of violence in Congress before the Civil War, tells Anna Diamond at *Smithsonian* she found at least 70 incidents of fighting among legislators, including a mass brawl in the House, though they often tried to paper over the conflicts. "It's all hidden between the lines in the Congressional record; it might say "the conversation became unpleasantly personal." That meant duel challenges, shoving, pulling guns and knives."

The better comparison, surprisingly, applies to post-WWII America. Despite periods where the U.S. political system and established political norms have been tested and stretched—the McCarthy hearings, Vietnam, Watergate, the Iraq War—partisan violence or attempts to subvert the system have been rare. But recent events, like changes to filibuster rules and other procedures in Congress as well as increasingly heated political rhetoric give Watts pause. "It is profoundly dangerous when a politician takes a step to undercut or ignore a political norm, it's extremely dangerous whenever anyone introduces violent rhetoric or actual violence into a republican system that's designed to promote compromise and consensus building."

The solution to keeping a republic healthy, if Rome can truly be a guide, is for the citizens to reject any attempts to alter these norms he says. "I think the lesson I take away most profoundly from spending so much time with these materials is basically, yes, we do need to assign blame to politicians and individuals who take a shortsighted view of the health of a republic in order to try to pursue their own personal objectives or specific short-term political advantages."

The example of the Roman Republic shows the result of not policing those norms and keeping violence in check is the potential loss of democracy. "No republic is eternal," Watts writes. "It lives only as long as its citizens want it. And, in both the 21st century A.D. and the first century B.C., when a republic fails to work as intended, its citizens are capable of choosing the stability of autocratic rule over the chaos of a broken republic."

Print Citations

CMS: Daley, Jason. "Lessons in the Decline of Democracy from the Ruined Roman Republic." In *The Reference Shelf: Democracy Evolving,* edited by Micah L. Issitt, 88-92. Amenia, NY: Grey House Publishing, 2019.

MLA: Daley, Jason. "Lessons in the Decline of Democracy frpom the Ruined Roman Republic." *The Reference Shelf: Democracy Evolving,* edited by Micah L. Issitt, Grey Housing Publishing, 2019, pp. 88-92.

APA: Daley, J. (2019). Lessons in the decline of democracy from the ruined Roman republic. In Micah L. Issitt (Ed.), *The reference shelf: Democracy evolving* (pp. 88-92). Amenia, NY: Grey Housing Publishing.

A Major Democracy Watchdog Just Published a Scathing Report on Trump

By Zack Beauchamp
Vox, February 5, 2019

A respected watchdog group on human rights is sounding the alarm: President Donald Trump poses an existential threat to American democracy, perhaps the greatest challenge it's seen in modern history.

> Trump has assailed essential institutions and traditions including the separation of powers, a free press, an independent judiciary, the impartial delivery of justice, safeguards against corruption, and most disturbingly, the legitimacy of elections," Freedom House president Mike Abramowitz writes in a special section of this year's report, released on Tuesday morning. "We cannot take for granted that institutional bulwarks against abuse of power will retain their strength, or that our democracy will endure perpetually. Rarely has the need to defend its rules and norms been more urgent.

Freedom House is a respected bipartisan watchdog group that compiles an annual report on the state of democracy and human rights around the world. This report, known as Freedom in the World, is widely cited by policymakers and academics who study democracy. It's a serious endeavor done by serious analysts—and this year, it's heavily focused on Trump.

The report has been paired with a full court press, including op-eds in the *Washington Post* and the *New York Times*, highlighting Freedom House's concern with the threat to American democracy under Trump. In essence, a nonpartisan human rights group is picking a major fight with the president.

This is an argument against the group's own interest. Roughly 85 percent of Freedom House's annual revenue comes from federal grants, per a 2016 audit report. If a vindictive Trump or his allies in Congress went after the organization, the consequences for its bottom line could be dire.

The fact that Abramowitz is willing to take that risk illustrates just how worried the group is about the survival of American democracy.

Why Freedom House Is Worried—And You Should Be Too

Freedom House's system ranks countries on a 0-to-100 scale, with 0 being fully authoritarian and 100 being perfectly democratic. Countries gain points based on the freedom of their elections, respect for basic rights like freedom of speech, the quality of their independent press, and other core liberal democratic rights.

The US, for all its problems, has historically done quite well on these metrics when compared to the rest of the world—scoring

> **Trump is following an established playbook from countries like Hungary and Venezuela where elected leaders have subverted their country's democracy.**

above 90 along with other advanced democracies. But its score has been in slow decline since 2009, due to things like the rise of hyperpartisan media, political polarization, and state-level restrictions on voting rights.

Then there was a noticeable dip in 2018, from 89 to 86, which Abramowitz attributes largely to Trump's influence. The US is currently below Italy, a fairly dysfunctional democracy with a governing coalition that currently includes the far-right Northern League.

"The total score of 86 still places the country firmly in the report's Free category, [but] the current overall US score puts American democracy closer to struggling counterparts like Croatia than to traditional peers such as Germany or the United Kingdom," he writes.

The reason this is so worrying, according to Abramowitz, is that Trump is following an established playbook from countries like Hungary and Venezuala where elected leaders have subverted their country's democracy. Trump's rhetorical and policy attacks happen to focus on the same institutions—the ones that help safeguard democracy.

"His attacks on the judiciary and the press, his resistance to anticorruption safeguards, and his unfounded claims of voting fraud by the opposition are all familiar tactics to foreign autocrats and populist demagogues who seek to subvert checks on their power," Abramowitz writes.

These tactics take time to work, and are most effective when there's limited public attention.

This is why, according to Abramowitz, it's important to sound the alarm now—before things start to get worse.

"The fact that the [US] system has proven durable so far is no guarantee that it will continue to do so," he writes. "Elsewhere in the world, in places like Hungary, Venezuela, or Turkey, Freedom House has watched as democratic institutions gradually succumbed to sustained pressure from an antidemocratic leadership, often after a halting start. Irresponsible rhetoric can be a first step toward real restrictions on freedom."

I'd encourage you to read the whole thing, to get a deeper sense of why it is that the authors see Trump as being uniquely threatening—the report goes into some detail on factors ranging from his attacks on the press as "the enemy of the people" to his systematic disregard for anti-corruption norms. But the short version is this: Freedom House is more than a little worried.

"Ours is a well-established and resilient democracy, and we can see the effect of its antibodies on the viruses infecting it," Abramowitz concludes. "Yet the pressure on our system is as serious as any experienced in living memory."

Print Citations

CMS: Beauchamp, Zack "A Major Democracy Watchdog Just Published a Scathing Report on Trump." In *The Reference Shelf: Democracy Evolving,* edited by Micah L. Issitt, 93-95. Amenia, NY: Grey House Publishing, 2019.

MLA: Beauchamp, Zack "A Major Democracy Watchdog Just Published a Scathing Report on Trump." *The Reference Shelf: Democracy Evolving,* edited by Micah L. Issitt, Grey Housing Publishing, 2019, pp. 93-95.

APA: Beauchamp, Z. (2019). A major democracy watchdog just published a scathing report on Trump. In Micah L. Issitt (Ed.), *The reference shelf: Democracy evolving* (pp. 93-95). Amenia, NY: Grey Housing Publishing.

Why Is American Democracy in Danger?

By Eric Schoon and Corey Pech
Washington Post, March 5, 2019

The United States is a flawed democracy. This is not a subjective statement, but rather a rating assigned to the United States by the Economist's annual Democracy Index. The downgrade from "full democracy" was the culmination of a decade of declining ratings, moving the United States out of a category that includes Australia, Canada and the United Kingdom and into a peer group with India, Botswana and Chile.

For decades following the successes of the civil rights movement and the passage of the 1965 Voting Rights Act, the United States had the basic ingredients that most analysts consider necessary for a functional democracy. Yet organizations that track levels of democracy around the world find that these ingredients are dwindling in the United States.

To understand why American democracy is declining, it is tempting to focus on recent events, such as the 2008 recession or state-level initiatives that restrict voting. But doing so risks mistaking symptoms of the problem for its causes. To drill down into the real causes of American decline, we should consider the conditions that have historically contributed to the collapse of democracies.

In fact, our current moment shares striking similarities with pre-World War II Europe, when the number of democracies was also shrinking rather than rising. In 1959, Seymour Martin Lipset, one of the 20th century's most prominent theorists of democracy, identified two broad factors as critical to explaining the differences between stable and unstable democracies during this period: economic development and political legitimacy.

In doing so, Lipset implicitly challenged some of the basic assumptions the Founding Fathers had made when creating the U.S. government. In *The Federalist Paper 10*, James Madison identified mob rule and the rise of political factions as the main causes of democratic failure, and so the framers of the U.S. Constitution attempted to limit the power of factions by building checks and balances into their political system. But Lipset believed these measures were insufficient for preventing factionalization and mob rule. He argued that strong factions will prevail in the presence of extreme economic inequality, regardless of how the political system itself is designed.

This is what had happened in many European countries during the 1920s and 1930s. Using indicators of economic development such as per capita income, number of doctors, number of telephones and radios and percentage of men in agriculture, Lipset showed in his analysis that there were stark differences in the overall levels of development between countries that had experienced an uninterrupted continuation of political democracy since World War I vs. those that had not. For example, the average per capita income across European countries that had maintained stable democracies was more than twice that of the countries that had experienced instability.

While Lipset's focus on the overall wealth and development of nations would not capture inequality today, at the time of his writing, more-developed countries were experiencing their highest degree of economic equality in history. His findings, thus, lent credence to his assertion that "a society divided between a large impoverished mass and a small favored elite would result either in oligarchy ... or in tyranny."

> **When it comes to economic development, then, the United States is increasingly accruing the conditions that destabilized democracies around the world before World War II.**

Today, Lipset's assessment still resonates. Despite decades of growing wealth, the United States has experienced rapid increases in economic and educational inequality. Wages in the United States have risen since 2000, but five times as fast for the highest earners than for the lowest earners. With fewer union protections and less government assistance, many Americans are struggling just to get by, even as the number of millionaires in the country hit record highs. A 2017 report by the U.S. Federal Reserve Board found that approximately 40 percent of Americans reported being unable to cover an unexpected $400 expense.

Lipset contended that education was also a key safeguard against factionalization and mob rule. That was one of the reasons economic development bolstered democracies: More-developed countries were better able to provide education. Here, too, though, the United States is falling short, with declining quality of education and growing inequality in educational attainment. As the education scholar Sean Reardon succinctly summarized in 2011: "The achievement gap between children from high- and low-income families is roughly 30 to 40 percent larger among children born in 2001 than among those born twenty-five years earlier."

Moreover, researchers have documented the increasing commodification of opportunities, showing that educational opportunities are increasingly dependent on the affluence and private resources of individual families.

When it comes to economic development, then, the United States is increasingly accruing the conditions that destabilized democracies around the world before World War II.

Nor is the United States doing well on Lipset's other marker of democratic health: the legitimacy of the political system. He identified specific conditions that would consistently undermine the legitimacy of democracy. First among these was the way that a society deals with major political conflicts. Lipset argued that a failure to resolve important political differences as they arose increased political polarization, because those differences would become embedded in conflicts between factions.

Indeed, much of the polarization and frustration in America can be linked to the failure to resolve fundamental cleavages. Debates over abortion rights, gun rights, access to health care, voting rights and other important social issues have amassed over the past half-century along increasingly partisan lines.

Political factionalization is not solely driven by failures to find solutions to thorny issues. Lipset argued that divisive politics thrived on social and intellectual isolation, which political leaders can manipulate to build support. Such leaders need to prevent their followers from being exposed to ideas and narratives that do not fit their political argument. Indeed, propaganda and claims of "fake news" were rampant in the European countries that experienced democratic decline in the interwar years.

In the U.S. context, we have seen such threats to legitimacy grow more prevalent during the past several decades. According to the Reuters Institute's 2017 analysis of people's news consumption habits across 37 countries, American news consumption is among the most polarized in the Western world. Viewed through the lens of Lipset's work, the intensification of ideological cleavages surrounding long-unresolved political issues, coupled with growing divisions over what kinds of news people consume and trust, have intensified the legitimacy crisis in the United States.

When it comes to the health of American democracy, Lipset's study paints a bleak picture. But it offers a reason for hope, as well. By directing our attention to the same social conditions that affected the stability of 20th century European democracies, his work highlights that voting citizens—not political institutions—are the key to stabilizing and rebuilding democracy. Our institutions may be weakening, but if our people are committed to a functioning democratic system, there is still reason to hope.

Print Citations

CMS: Schoon, Eric, and Corey Pech. "Why Is American Democracy in Danger?" In *The Reference Shelf: Democracy Evolving*, edited by Micah L. Issitt, 96-98. Amenia, NY: Grey House Publishing, 2019.

MLA: Schoon, Eric, and Corey Pech. "Why Is American Democracy in Danger? *The Reference Shelf: Democracy Evolving*, edited by Micah L. Issitt, Grey Housing Publishing, 2019, pp. 96-98.

APA: Schoon, E., & Pech, C. (2019). Why is American democracy in danger? In Micah L. Issitt (Ed.), *The reference shelf: Democracy evolving* (pp. 96-98). Amenia, NY: Grey Housing Publishing.

4

How Fragile is Democracy?

By Zorro2212, via Wikimedia

The European Union has accused Poland, particularly the ruling nationalist Law and Justice party, of undermining the rule of law and restricting free speech. A KOD (Komitet Obrony Demokracji, or Committee for the Defence of Democracy) demonstration in Warsaw against the ruling Law and Justice party, May 2016.

The Global View

The perception of a crisis in American democracy coincides with similar concerns in many countries with democratic systems. A rise in global far right activism is one of the causes for this global concern, in addition to the nationalist and populist movements that have swept through some democratic nations, eroding democratic freedoms with the introduction of authoritarianism. There is a growing perception that the democratic nations of the world must do more to promote and protect the global democratic community. Despite concern over democracy's future, by some standards, democratic governments are thriving more than ever in the twenty-first century, and the innate appeal of democracy has enabled it to spread, marginally, through much of the world. Whether democracy is the future of global society, however, is a question that cannot be answered. Some political analysts believe that democracy, as a human ideal, is more fragile than is widely believed. The debate over the future of global democracy can be examined by looking at the last period in which Americans were actively promoting the large scale export of democracy, the decades-long Cold War.

Echoes of the Cold War

During the Cold War, Americans perceived a global struggle for the future of democracy, one in which the United States and its allies in Western Europe were competing with the former Soviet Union and China. This was a period of ideological colonialism in which nations envisioning themselves as bastions of democracy competed with those representing communism to spread their ideological visions to as many of the world's developing nations as possible. The Korean War and the Vietnam War became two of the most violent events linked to this ideological struggle, but it was a contest that also saw violent conflict in the Middle East, Africa, and Central and South America.

Many American political analysts, chiefly those with a more conservative or nationalistic bent, believe that the United States and its allied democratic powers won the Cold War with the collapse of the former Soviet Union in 1991. For instance, Arnold Beichman wrote in a 2001 article for the *Hoover Institution*, "There is no Soviet Power; it's 'bloated and unhealthy limits' have been retracted without bloodshed. There isn't even a Soviet Union. So didn't the democracies win the cold war?"[1] Beichman is able to claim victory in the Cold War by greatly limiting the parameters that might be used to define it. Even simply considering the fate of the allegedly failed Soviet State, there is little evidence of a victory. The former Soviet Union rebounded from its collapse and has again become an aggressive international actor. Though U.S. politicians continue to debate the validity of any Russian threat, the Russian state's intentions were made clear by their effort to undermine America's democracy by interfering in the 2016 elections with a blend of propaganda and fake social media manipulation.[2] China, America's other primary enemy in the Cold War, has risen to become the world's second largest economy, in many ways growing faster than the United States, and it has achieved this without adopting a democratic government. China's authoritarian capitalist system is working well enough, and it has begun a more aggressive era of international economic colonialism, building economic bridges to countries in Africa and the Middle East that have been largely ignored by America, and exporting their version of capitalist ideology, a version that still hinges on authoritarian communism, to the rest of the world.[3]

The deeper failures of the Cold War can be better understood by looking at the fate of nations that became proxy battlegrounds for America, the Soviet Union, or China. Despite the fact that the collapse of the Soviet states led to a brief respite from the fear of Soviet aggression in the United States, the Bush and Clinton administrations did little to foster a strong network of democratic states. Instead, America reduced its involvement with the nascent democratic states that it had sought to foster from the 1950s through the 1980s. With the proxy conflict among the great powers at a temporary standstill, countries like Nicaragua, El Salvador, Afghanistan, and the Congo suffered as various factions competed for power. Radical right-wing groups formerly on the fringes of society became major military powers and this led to the establishment of violent dictatorships. America's Cold War military activities fueled the rise of authoritarian regimes that later became problems for the United States, creating decades of war.

The "War on Terror" provides a direct example of how the United States lost in the Cold War. Saddam Hussein, a man who came to power because his regime received direct support from the Central Intelligence Agency and the U.S. government, placed Iraq under a violent dictatorship and later became the target of a multibillion-dollar, decades-long effort to undo the regime that the United States helped to create. Meanwhile, the radical right-wing Islamist group known as the Taliban took full control of Afghanistan, a nation that was one of the key proxy battlegrounds between the United States and the Soviet Union in the 1980s.[4] At the same time, the United States continued to have perhaps its greatest impact on the world through the spread of U.S. popular culture, in the form of music, movies, and attitudes about cultural values. Within the violent regimes in Afghanistan, Iraq, and elsewhere, resentment against the United States and Western culture festered, as radical right-wing leaders perceived the encroachment of U.S. culture on their own traditionalist values. Eventually, radical right-wing militant groups achieved sufficient resources to attack the great powers directly, resulting in the 9/11 terrorist attacks. The U.S. government pursued a reactionary agenda intended to assuage fears but based on insufficient long-term strategy. The result was a decades-long war in Iraq, Afghanistan, and eventually Syria.[5]

Even if claims of a U.S. victory in the Cold War can be treated with significant skepticism, there is likewise little evidence to claim that the communist powers fared much better. States propped up by communist regimes likewise fell into poverty and instability. North Korea, which was created by a combination of Chinese support and the threat of U.S. nuclear aggression, has developed into a dismal economy and a largely stagnant culture. Leftist communist and socialist revolutions in Central America also resulted in fragile, struggling states dominated by military dictatorships. There were no clear winners in the Cold War, and the era can best be remembered as a series of cautionary examples regarding the dangers inherent to nation building, practices that rarely result in stable societies.

The State of Global Democracy

What is the state of democracy in the global sphere? It is a question without clear answers. From a certain perspective, democracy appears to be thriving on the global scale. Democratic governments outnumber other forms of government, and the spread of capitalism has led to democratic reforms in many countries. However, the organization Freedom House released a report on the state of world democracy in 2019 indicating that, globally, for the thirteenth straight year, there was a "decline in global freedom." Among the signs for concern cited by researchers at the organization was the decline of democratic freedoms in many formerly stable democracies. For instance, the former democracy of Venezuela evolved into an autocratic military dictatorship. Similarly, the former democracy of Turkey, once seen as a bastion of Islamic democracy, likewise lapsed into a military dictatorship under nationalist ideologue Tayyip Erdogan. In both Venezuela and Turkey, democratic watchdogs and researchers have reported that the autocratic governments have consolidated their power by misusing military and police powers to eliminate the free press and to imprison political opponents.

Another cause for concern with regard to the state of global democracy has been the rise of populist nationalism. While the United States again serves as an example, the imposition of authoritarian nationalism is more pronounced in Hungary and Poland. Both nations were democracies that transitioned from Soviet-dominated communism, but they have since declined into semi-fascist states in which powerful governmental authorities have limited the freedom of the press and curtailed legal protections to consolidate power behind traditionalist conservative agendas. The emergence of authoritarian nationalism has not only been viewed as a sign of democratic decline, but also presents a threat to (and is partially inspired by) the movement toward international governance, most prominently represented by the formation of the European Union.[6]

In April of 2019, the Council on Foreign Relations reported on another study from the University of Gothenburg based on results from the "V-Dem," or "Varieties of Democracy," project, finding that the global "third wave of autocratization" is more pronounced than even researchers at Freedom House perceived in 2018 and is impacting more democracies. Utilizing a multidimensional dataset of indicators to judge the strength of democratic governments, the researchers found that the current shift toward autocracy actually began in the mid-1990s and is marked by "gradual regressions" such as subtle legal shifts and flawed elections that reduced citizen control over their governments while increasing the control of minority interest groups. The study found that many states have shifted toward autocracy due to the deterioration of democratic protections rather than through a coup or other large-scale shift.[7] One example can be found in the United States, where gerrymandering has resulted in electoral districts that bear less and less resemblance to popular will, enabling candidates representing certain groups to win elections without popular support.

However, the decline in global democracy perceived by some political analysts is neither total nor complete. Democratic governments remain more common than any other form of government, and Freedom House has identified a number of societies in which legitimate democratic reforms have occurred. This reflects what researchers have characterized as the "real and powerful" promise of democracy and its "enduring appeal as a means of holding leaders accountable and creating the conditions for a better life."[8] Regions in which democratic governance has strengthened present opportunities for democratic coalitions and cooperation, collectively strengthening global democracy through multinational engagement. But such efforts are possible only when nations like the United States embrace potential roles in the international community. Under the Trump administration, America has seen a sharp withdrawal from international participation, reflecting Trump's "America First" foreign policy agenda. A majority of Americans, however, still perceive an important role for the United States on the global stage, and this means that it is possible for the United States to engage more deeply in this process in the future.

Works Used

Abramowitz, Michael J. and Wendell L. Willkie II. "We Looked at the State of Democracy around the World, and the Results Are Grim." *The Washington Post.* Jan 17, 2018. Retrieved from https://www.washingtonpost.com/news/democracy-post/wp/2018/01/17/we-looked-at-the-state-of-democracy-around-the-world-and-the-results-are-grim/?utm_term=.b71e1af30fef.

Beichman, Arnold. "Who Won the Cold War?" *Hoover Institution.* Jul 2, 2001. Retrieved from https://www.hoover.org/research/who-won-cold-war.

Brands, Hal. "China's Master Plan: Exporting an Ideology." *Bloomberg.* Jun 11, 2018. Retrieved from https://www.bloomberg.com/opinion/articles/2018-06-11/china-s-master-plan-exporting-an-ideology.

"Democracy in Retreat." *Freedom House.* Freedom in the World 2019. Retrieved from https://freedomhouse.org/report/freedom-world/freedom-world-2019/democracy-in-retreat.

Gopal, Anand. "How the US Created the Afghan War—and Then Lost It." *The Nation.* Apr 29, 2014. Retrieved from https://www.thenation.com/article/how-us-created-afghan-war-and-then-lost-it/.

Kurlantzick, Joshua. "The State of Global Democracy Today Is Even Worse Than It Looks: V-Demo's New Democracy Research." *Council on Foreign Relations.* Apr 3, 2019. Retrieved from https://www.cfr.org/blog/state-global-democracy-today-even-worse-it-looks-v-dems-new-democracy-research.

Westad, Odd Arne. "The Cold War and America's Delusion of Victory." *The New York Times.* Aug 28, 2017. Retrieved from https://www.nytimes.com/2017/08/28/opinion/cold-war-american-soviet-victory.html.

Wheeler, Marcy. "What Mueller's Reminder about Russian Interference Really Meant." *The Washington Post*. May 30, 2019. https://www.washingtonpost.com/outlook/2019/05/30/what-muellers-reminder-about-russian-interference-really-meant/?noredirect=on&utm_term=.03ea5acc0b33.

Notes

1. Beichman, "Who Won the Cold War?"
2. Wheeler, "What Mueller's Reminder about Russian Interference Really Meant."
3. Brands, "China's Master Plan: Exporting an Ideology."
4. Gopal, "How the US Created the Afghan War—and Then Lost It."
5. Westad, "The Cold War and America's Delusion of Victory."
6. Abramowitz and Willkie, "We Looked at the State of Democracy around the World, and the Results Are Grim."
7. Kurlantzick, "The State of Global Democracy Today Is Even Worse Than It Looks: V-Dem's New Democracy Research."
8. "Democracy in Retreat," *Freedom House*.

The Growing Signs of the Fragility and Resilience of Liberal Democracy

By Heidi Koolmeister
Diplomaatia Magazine, International Centre for Defence and Security, March 1, 2019

As we celebrate the 30th anniversary of the fall of the Berlin Wall in 1989, it would be fitting to assess the current state of liberal democracy on a global level in order to understand in what direction the world is evolving. It seems that in recent years the success of liberal democracy has come to halt and it has started going into decline while authoritarian regimes are emerging, both in established Western democracies and the world in general. We are witnessing decreasing support for democratic states, human and civil rights, and the principles of the rule of law; and the increasing popularity of illiberal populism and nationalism and the growing strength of authoritarian regimes around the world. The future of liberal democracy seems to be getting bleaker with every passing year. This raises the questions whether liberal democracy is capable of facing down the challenges of today: how can we define, evaluate and measure its resilience?; what makes some democracies more durable than others?; and why do some countries experience the erosion of democratic qualities, backsliding from democracy, or even its total failure? By understanding these issues we can consider the fragility of liberal democracy better and increase its resilience to adapt to today's changes, challenges and crises.

Liberal Democracy in Crisis

After the collapse of the Soviet Union, many new democratic countries stepped onto the world stage. This seemed to confirm that democracy would soon become the main form of governance. Samuel Huntington described it in 1991 as a "third wave" of democratisation that started in 1974.[1] Even though many of those new democracies took hold, a number of "third wave" democracies remained essentially unfree. Leonardo Morlino defined them as "hybrid regimes",[2] Steven Levitsky and Lucan Way as "competitive authoritarian regimes"[3] and Thomas Carothers as "gray-zone countries".[4] Thus, it is safe to say that "third wave" democracies are very different in terms of the quality of their democracy.

Today it can be seen that the quality of democracy is declining in many countries due to both internal and external influences. IDEA's (International Institute for Democracy and Electoral Assistance) 2017 report "The Global State of Democracy: Exploring Democracy's Resilience" highlighted that many such "third wave" democracies have problems with re-consolidation and democratic backsliding.[5] This phenomenon has also been called "the erosion of democracy" (Huntington,[6] Marc Plattner[7]), "democratic recession" (Larry Diamond),[8] and crisis of democracy or disintegration or decline of democracy (IDEA).

Diamond, one of the leading researchers at Stanford University in the field of democratisation, has estimated that the decline in democracy can be traced back to 2006. First, crises in democratic regimes have become significantly more common since then; second, the overall quality or stability of democracy has declined; third, authoritarianism has spread; and fourth, states with advanced democracies are not functioning well and they lack the will to promote and protect democracy abroad effectively (Diamond, 147–8). These signs of the increasing fragility of democracy mean

> **The resilience of democracy is an internal characteristic that, while it can be supported by external actors, must be primarily developed from within.**

that, when faced with the changes, challenges and crises that could push a democratic regime over the edge towards authoritarianism, a state's resilience is crucial for its survival. At the same time, we lack knowledge about the resilience or fragility of democratic regimes and the internal working mechanism of this phenomenon. A better understanding of this would give us the opportunity to support the resilience of democratic states when they face internal or external changes, challenges or crises.

Resilience and Fragility of Democratic Regimes

In order to better understand the resilience of a democratic regime and its defining and characteristic features, we need to define what resilience is. Resilience comes from the Latin *resiliens*, which literally means "rebounding". This shows that the basis of the concept of resilience is the capability of a strained body to recover its size and shape after deformation caused especially by compressive stress (Merriam-Webster dictionary). In the 2017 IDEA report, Timothy Sisk describes the resilience of democracy as "the properties of a political system to cope, survive and recover from complex challenges and crises that represent stresses or pressures that can lead to a systemic failure".[9]

Thus, resilience is an internal quality of democratic regimes, and durable regimes are characterised by the following features: *flexibility*—the ability to absorb stress or pressure; *recovery*—the ability to overcome challenges or crises; *adaptation*—the ability to change in response to a stress to the system; and *innovation*—the ability to change in a way that more efficiently or effectively addresses the challenge or crisis.[5] At the same time, elsewhere[9] Sisk seems to ignore the original meaning of resilience or endurance that was encompassed by *resiliens*—the ability to adapt but return to the original point of equilibrium that can be characterised by "democratic identity" and "regime continuity" when the regime faces internal or external changes, challenges or crises. Hence, the resilience or endurance of a regime can be described as the ability of the system to adapt to change to a certain degree before the identity of the system transforms into another type of regime, while in order for the regime to be resilient, it should keep its democratic identity and maintain its continuity.

Fragility is the opposite of resilience. It comes from the Latin *fragilis*, which means subjecting to or being susceptible to breakage or fracture (Merriam-Webster). Thus, a regime can be either resilient or fragile: while resilient or durable democratic regimes have internal mechanisms that help them cope with change, challenges and crises, fragile regimes do not have the same capabilities and are more susceptible to decline in the quality of democracy, to crisis, or to the disintegration of democracy. As Sisk has stated, such fragility can be seen more often in "'partial' or grey-zone democracies, 'competitive authoritarian regimes' or hybrid democracies in autocratic states, which can be stable",[5] or consolidated democracies, since states that are transitioning to a democratic regime are more fragile in comparison to consolidated democratic regimes.

Endurance, Continuity and Persistence of Democracy

It can be stated that democratic regimes have generally turned out to be quite durable throughout history, but this has been undervalued since the success of democracy has not been global. Plattner has stated that focusing on the persistence of authoritarian regimes has caused the endurance of democracy to be undervalued or ignored.[10] In his view, democracies have endured remarkably well and the third wave of democratisation, which started in 1974, has not yet gone into reverse, i.e., the number of states experiencing the collapse of democracy has not exceeded the number of new democracies, even though Huntington (1991 has stated that previous waves of democratisation have receded sooner or later. According to Plattner, this is due to the fact that democratic regimes have a greater legitimacy in the eyes of not only their citizens but also the wider world.10 This internal quality of democratic regimes has been also discussed through other similar concepts, such as the continuity,[11] endurance[12] and persistence (Burnell, P., Calvert, P. (1999). "Democracy: Persistent Practice or Durable Idea?" *Democratization*, 6:1, pp. 271-84.) of democracies in academic literature. Hence, despite citizens' dissatisfaction with the quality and performance of democracy, advanced democracies still display remarkable endurance. The same has been stated by Levitsky and Way,[13] who support the statement that "third wave" democracies have turned out to be surprisingly durable and survived in countries where conditions are extremely unfavourable, for example in places with a deficient or non-existent tradition of democratic rule, in weak states with widespread poverty and inequality, and in divided societies. They have also endured serious economic crises and radical economic reforms, which many academics have never considered compatible with democracy.

Growing Signs of Fragility in Liberal Democracies

At the same time, there are today clear signs of the growing fragility of liberal democracy and the crisis of liberal democracy on a global level. This has been accompanied by the weakening of human rights and civil liberties, the erosion of democratic norms and an increase in populism and nationalism—both in so-called transition countries and established Western democracies. According to the Freedom House report for 2018, democracy has been in recession in 71 countries and there were positive developments in only 35.[14] This marks the 12th consecutive year in which Freedom House has documented the decline of global democracy. The Economist Intelligence Unit also reported the decline of democracy at the global level in 2017, stressing in particular the worrying developments connected with freedom of speech and the media.[15] According to World Values Survey data, decreasing support for democracy and increasing support for non-democratic forms of governance can be also seen in countries with developed democracies.[16]

We can see this happening in Europe, where populist and nationalist parties have emerged and risen to power, e.g., in Austria, Hungary, Italy and Poland. It can therefore be predicted that both right- and left-wing extremist populist and nationalist political forces will make progress in national elections in EU member states in 2019 and the forthcoming elections to the European parliament. At the same time, Europe is not the only region where populism and nationalism have triumphed. For example, in countries with liberal democracies such as the US and Brazil there has been a decline in the quality or stability of democracy, and in the case of illiberal democracies such as the Philippines and Turkey authoritarian elements have gained a stronger foothold.

Many of these countries have faced political, economic or social challenges such as immigration pressure and problems following the economic crisis, which have posed a threat to the legitimacy of liberal democracy. In many such countries, public support for the government and traditional political institutions has declined. This has in turn increased the support for external and anti-establishment political forces. Thus, we can often see that the biggest threat to liberal democracies results from democratic mechanisms such as regular elections, which are the cornerstone of a democratic system. In many of the aforementioned countries with advanced democracies, illiberal populist and nationalist political actors have come to power through elections and it can be seen that the political parties that have undermined the regime of liberal democracies have done so as a result of a learning process, observing and copying similar developments in other countries to gain power.

Such challenges have caused the gradual decline, erosion and/or backsliding of the quality of democracy both in the Western European countries with advanced democracies and in the so-called "third wave" democracies all over the world, including democratic post-communist states. Support for authoritarian forces is increasing in transition countries that do not have a tradition of democracy or have only a recent one. Driven by those developments, authoritarian regimes such as in China and Russia are acting increasingly forcefully in the international stage, as they can find like-minded allies more easily in order to achieve their strategic goals both in bilateral relations and in multilateral forums. Growing signs of the fragility of liberal democracy show that we have entered a new era since the end of the Cold War in which the erosion of democracy, human rights and fundamental freedoms can be acutely felt, and thus the challenges facing liberal democracy are the biggest they have been in the past 30 years.

The Role of the EU in Promoting and Protecting the Resilience of Democracy at the Global Level

In addition to identifying the internal mechanisms of democracy, external actors can and must promote and protect democracy. In the EU's Global Strategy on Foreign and Security Policy—the so-called Global Strategy adopted in 2016 as a framework for EU activity around the world—the Union focused on supporting resilience both within itself and in third countries.[17] In the strategy, resilience is defined as "a broader concept encompassing all individuals and the whole of society ... featuring democracy, trust in institutions, and sustainable development". The basis of the global strategy is thus the notion that a durable state is a democratic state, since the shortcomings in democracy based on the principles of human rights and the rule of law endanger the opportunities of a state and society for sustainable development.

The EU has thus set a goal to use its external activities to strengthen the resilience of states or their ability to adapt to political, economic, environmental, demographic or social pressure and to support their ability to preserve their main functions under pressure in a way that would guarantees democracy, the rule of law, and fundamental and human rights.[18] At the same time, reduced efficiency, energy and confidence in promoting and protecting democracy and fighting against democratic backsliding is evident in the case of both the EU and the US.[19] The protection of liberal democracy against an authoritarian decline as well as the resilience and further progress of global democracy depend on the actions of the EU today. Hence, it is important that the EU—both the Union and individual member states—continue to protect and promote democracy and human rights in their foreign policy in a uniform way in order to support the resilience of states to counter today's changes, challenges and crises and those in the future.

The endurance of democracy depends on both internal and external factors and influences, but since it is an internal characteristic, internal factors and influences are decisive in whether a regime will be durable or fragile in a situation in which it is influenced by both internal and external changes, challenges and crises. At the same time, external actors like the EU can have a positive effect on the internal resilience of democracy. If international actors such as the EU prevent the risk of democratic reversal and intervene at the right time using appropriate foreign-policy measures, the erosion or decline of the quality of democracy might not occur and the country may turn out to be resilient. At the same time, it is important to stress that the resilience of democracy is an internal characteristic that, while it can be supported by external actors, must be primarily developed from within. This is why it is particularly important to support the establishment and maintenance of democratic governments in third countries and support a civil society that protects democracy, fundamental rights and freedoms at the state level.

[1] Huntington, S. P. *The Third Wave: Democratization in the Late Twentieth Century*. Norman, OK and London: University of Oklahoma Press, 1991.

[2] Morlino, L. *Changes for Democracy: Actors, Structures, Processes*. Oxford: Oxford University Press, 2011.

[3] Levitsky, S. and Way, L. *Competitive Authoritarianism: Hybrid Regimes After the Cold War*. New York: Cambridge University Press, 2010.

[4] Carothers, T. "The End of the Transition Paradigm". *Journal of Democracy* 13(1) (2002), pp. 5–21.

[5] Sisk, T. D. "Democracy's resilience in a changing world" in IDEA, "The Global State of Democracy: Exploring Democracy's Resilience". Stockholm: International IDEA, 2017.

[6] Huntington, S. P. "Democracy for the Long Haul". *Journal of Democracy* 7(2) (1996), pp. 3–13.

[7] Plattner, M. F. "Populism, Pluralism, and Liberal Democracy". *Journal of Democracy* 21(1) (2010), pp. 81–92.

[8] Diamond, L. "Facing Up to the Democratic Recession". *Journal of Democracy* 26(1) (2015), pp. 141–55.

[9] Sisk, T. D. "Democracy and Resilience: Conceptual Approaches and Considerations". Background Paper. Stockholm: International IDEA, 2017.

[10] Plattner, "Populism, Pluralism, and Liberal Democracy", p. 82.

[11] Przeworski, A. *Sustainability of Democracy*. Cambridge: Cambridge University Press, 1995.

[12] Cheibub, J. A., Przeworski, A., Limongi Neto, F. and Alvarez, M. "What Makes Democracies Endure?" *Journal of Democracy* 7(1) (1996), pp. 39–55.

[13] Levitsky, S. and Way, L. "The Myth of Democratic Recession". *Journal of Democracy* 26(1) (2015), pp. 45–58 [55–6].

[14] Freedom House. "Freedom in the World 2018: Democracy in Crisis". freedomhouse.org/sites/default/files/FH_FITW_Repor...

[15] The Economist Intelligence Unit. www.eiu.com.

[16] World Values Survey. www.worldvaluessurvey.org/wvs.jsp.

[17] European Union. "Shared vision, common action: A stronger Europe. A Global Strategy for the European Union's Foreign and Security Policy", 2016. Available at europa.eu/globalstragegy/en/global-strategy-...

[18] European External Action Service. Joint Communication to the European Parliament and to the Council. "A Strategic Approach to Resilience in the EU's external action", June 2017. eeas.europa.eu/headquarters/headquarters-homepage_...

[19] Diamond, "Facing Up to the Democratic Recession", 152–3.

Print Citations

CMS: Koolmeister, Heidi. "The Growing Signs of the Fragility and Resilience of Liberal Democracy." In *The Reference Shelf: Democracy Evolving,* edited by Micah L. Issitt, 107-112. Amenia, NY: Grey House Publishing, 2019.

MLA: Koolmeister, Heidi. "The Growing Signs of the Fragility and Resilience of Liberal Democracy." *The Reference Shelf: Democracy Evolving,* edited by Micah L. Issitt, Grey Housing Publishing, 2019, pp. 107-112.

APA: Koolmeister, H. (2019). The growing signs of the fragility and resilience of liberal democracy. In Micah L. Issitt (Ed.), *The reference shelf: Democracy evolving* (pp. 107-112). Amenia, NY: Grey Housing Publishing.

"Yes, We Need to Do Better": World Leaders Talk Democracy

The New York Times, September 20, 2017

At the Athens Democracy Forum, a conference convened by *The New York Times* in Athens, from Sept. 13 to 17, global leaders talked about the state of democracy and its challenges around the world. The following are edited excerpts from several of the participants, who discussed the relevancy of international organizations like the United Nations, how to better engage young people in the democratic process, policy strategies can help bring democracy to the developing world and what are some new models to consider.

Amina Mohamed, *Minister of foreign affairs and international trade, Kenya*

I know there's no way we would have resolved in the Horn of Africa the issue of piracy if the international community did not come together. There's no way we'd deal with the issues in Somalia of terrorism if the international community did not come together. Look at the bird flu. If the World Health Organization did not rise to the occasion, I think we would have a pandemic of major proportions that would have engulfed all of the earth. Ebola, if the European Union and the United Nations did not come together as an international community and send in the many thousands of young health workers, I don't think that would have been resolved. Yes, we need to do better, but I do not think that we should rule multilateralism and international cooperation out. It's created the space that we need for dialogue, for discussions, for effective decision-making.

Kevin Rudd, *Former prime minister of Australia and president of the Asia Society Policy Institute*

The global political leadership is so utterly consumed in holding together the simple fabric of their local democracies and local economies, that their capacity, their attention span, their ability to sustain the existing institutions of global governance, from the United Nations, from the Bretton Woods Institutions and the rest, is itself going down. The net effectiveness of global institutions is being challenged because they are not delivering the goods. Look at the U.N. What's the hallmark achievement of the U.N. in the last couple of years? You could say the Paris agreement on climate change. The other big achievement is the Sustainable Development Goals—Agenda 2030. I do not see any hope of the current U.N. machinery

> **You can't have a democracy if you don't have informed citizens—citizens who have critical thinking.**

in the way it's structured, or the way in which nation states are providing it with political and financial support, to deliver on Agenda 2030. It is a ticking time bomb for the legitimacy of the U.N. system if the Sustainable Development Goals are not delivered. States increasingly perceive the U.N. as ineffective. What I worry about is death by a thousand cuts to the U.N. Unless we radically turn this around, you will see it slowly drift to occupying the margins of global irrelevance.

Brian Smith, *President of the Coca-Cola Company's Europe, Middle East and Africa group*

The social contract, whatever that ends up becoming, whatever those important issues are for the communities the businesses work in, if it does not become a part of what corporations do and what we invest in, then consumers will eventually drop us. It's almost part of survival into the next generation. If we don't do it ourselves, then there should probably be ways in which we are forced to do that through entities and constituencies that would push us in that direction.

Kerry Kennedy, *President of Robert F. Kennedy Human Rights*

When I started working in human rights in the early 1980s, all of Latin America was under right-wing military dictatorships. Today, there's not one that's left standing. All of Eastern Europe was under Communism. And today, there's not a Communist government left. South Africa was under the height of apartheid, and South Africa has had a series of freely elected governments elected by a majority of its people. Women's rights was not on the international agenda. Today, the women's rights convention has been ratified by 183 countries. All those changes happened not because governments wanted them to, but because small groups of determined people harnessed the dream of freedom and made it come true. That's what changes the world.

Irina Bokova, *Director-General of UNESCO*

There is a big social movement. The young generation is part of this and strongly pushing against inequalities and injustice. But we should hold governments accountable. I think governments should be there in the debate. I think education is the key to many issues. It's about skills, jobs, values and human rights education. It's about democracy at the end of the day. You can't have a democracy if you don't have informed citizens—citizens who have critical thinking. It is critical to have this young generation as global citizens.

Roby Senderowitsch, *Practice manager, Governance Global Practice, World Bank*

Countries have evolved in a way that they try to take the best from the different models that they can find. When it comes to competitiveness and industrialization, maybe they look at China. When they look at innovation and how new technologies can help foster growth in their countries, they look at India or Ireland today. It's a combination of different models. There are some people who say a dictatorship is much better than a democratic system to get there. This is a false premise, and there is not enough evidence to sustain it. It's much better to live in an imperfect democracy than a perfect dictatorship. Even in a perfect dictatorship you need to be very lucky, to choose the right dictator, which is a paradox by itself because you don't choose your dictators.

Sergei Guriev, *Chief economist, European Bank for Reconstruction and Development*

Part of the electoral setbacks in the West in 2016 were about people who felt they were being left behind. And it's not just about inequality. Working in Central and Western Europe, we know that some equality can be unfair. It is unfair if I work harder, like in the Soviet system, and I don't get compensated for that. But there is unfair inequality where we have inequality of opportunity, lack of shared prosperity, lack of inclusion. And this is where Nordic countries are delivering much better than some other Western countries. And that makes their political systems more sustainable and robust.

Keboitse Machangana, *Director of Global Programs, International Institute for Democracy and Electoral Assistance*

More and more people are voting than before. We have more and more countries that are characterized as democracies. What is being challenged right now is not whether democracy is right or wrong. I think we have passed that debate. I think what we are seeing in the world is now people wanting better quality democracy. They would like to see that democracy being practiced exactly the way they believe it should be. When leaders are coming up with policies for problems, do they take into account the views of the people into those issues? What we are seeing around the world, the social movements, the student protests, is people saying they want to be engaged whether there's an election or not. Democracy needs to go back to basics: the rule of the people.

He Jiahong, *Director of the Center for Anti-Corruption and Rule of Law, the School of Law, Renmin University of China*

At the end of the 1970s, China didn't know the term "rule of law." We just tried to restore the legal system. We thought we could learn something from Western countries about democracy, but democracy cannot be exported. We have to find our own way. We should push forward rule of law first as a basis for development of democracy. And for development of democracy, we should have gradual changes. I don't like the word "revolution" anymore. I like the word "evolution," so people may have the right to know first, and then the right to speak, and then the right to vote.

Print Citations

CMS: "'Yes, 'We Need to Do Better': World Leaders Talk Democracy." In *The Reference Shelf: Democracy Evolving*, edited by Micah L. Issitt, 113-116. Amenia, NY: Grey House Publishing, 2019.

MLA: "'Yes, 'We Need to Do Better': World Leaders Talk Democracy." *The Reference Shelf: Democracy Evolving*, edited by Micah L. Issitt, Grey Housing Publishing, 2019, pp. 113-116.

APA: The New York Times. (2019). "Yes we need to do better": World leaders talk democracy. In Micah L. Issitt (Ed.), *The reference shelf: Democracy evolving* (pp. 113-116). Amenia, NY: Grey Housing Publishing.

Despite Global Concerns about Democracy, More Than Half of Countries Are Democratic

By Drew DeSilver
Pew Research Center, May 14, 2019

Concern has been growing for the past several years about the future of democracy, and there is considerable dissatisfaction in many countries with how democracy is working in practice. But public support for democratic ideals remains strong, and by one measure, global democracy is at or near a modern-day high.

As of the end of 2017, 96 out of 167 countries with populations of at least 500,000 (57%) were democracies of some kind, and only 21 (13%) were autocracies. Nearly four dozen other countries—46, or 28%—exhibited elements of both democracy and autocracy. Broadly speaking, the share of democracies among the world's governments has been on an upward trend since the mid-1970s, and now sits just shy of its post-World War II record (58% in 2016).

To track the spread of democracy around the globe, we used the ratings contained in the Center for Systemic Peace's Polity IV dataset. Polity is a widely used resource in political science that analyzes and codes how political authority is gained and used in every fully independent state with a population of 500,000 or more (167 of the world's 200 or so sovereign states in the current version).

Polity assesses six key factors, from openness of political participation to constraints on the chief executive, to place each country on a 21-point scale ranging from +10 ("consolidated democracy") to –10 ("hereditary monarchy"). It doesn't rate countries whose central government has collapsed or those subject to foreign intervention or occupation. In 2017, there were three countries in the former group (Libya, Yemen and South Sudan) and one in the latter (Bosnia and Herzegovina).

Following the Polity guidelines, we categorized all countries scoring from +6 to +10 as democracies, those from –6 to –10 as autocracies and everything in between as "mixed." We then tracked the changing prevalence of democracy and autocracy over the seven decades since the end of the Second World War.

In 2017, 33 countries were considered fully consolidated democracies, with a Polity rating of +10. The peak postwar year for consolidated democracies was 2006, when there were 35; since then, two (Belgium and the United States) have slipped from the top tier.

Belgium fell 2 points, to +8, following its June 2007 parliamentary election, which deepened divisions between the country's French- and Flemish-speaking communities and sparked a long-running political crisis that at times threatened to split the country. The United States was docked 2 points in 2016 due to an increase in "factional competition," and now also sits at +8. The Polity researchers noted that "political discourse in the United States had become increasingly partisan" during Barack Obama's administration, and that Donald Trump "used combative rhetoric to excite 'populist' support and seize the Republican Party nomination." Trump's "surprise" Electoral College victory, they added, "polarized political competition into 'anti-establishment' and 'anti-Trump' factions."

In 1977, only 35 of the 143 countries rated by Polity (24%) qualified as democracies, while 89 (62%) were classified as autocracies of one stripe or another (including nine absolute hereditary monarchies). Although the number of democracies began edging higher in subsequent years and the number of autocracies gradually fell, half of the Polity-rated countries were still considered autocracies as recently as 1988.

But democracy spread rapidly as the Cold War ended and the Soviet-led bloc—and eventually the Soviet Union itself —crumbled between 1989 and 1991. Of the 75 countries rated as autocracies in 1987, only 15 (20%) were still rated that way three decades later. More than a third (27) had become democracies, and most of the rest had mixed ratings. (One, Libya, was not rated in 2017 because of regime instability, and five other states had ceased to exist.) Among 30 new nations formed since 1987, 17 were rated as democracies in 2017, six were autocracies, four were mixed and three were not rated due to instability or foreign intervention.

> **The share of democracies among the world's governments has been on an upward trend since the mid-1970s, and now sits just shy of its post-World War II record.**

Polity's democracy ratings are by no means the only ones out there, though because of differing methodologies they tell somewhat different stories. Freedom House, for instance, rates 86 out of 195 countries (44%) as "free," using criteria that include both political and civil rights. And though nearly half of the 167 countries in the Economist Intelligence Unit's Democracy Index are considered to be some form of democracy, only 12% (20) are rated as "full democracies"; nearly a third (55 countries) are counted as "flawed democracies" —including the U.S.

Although our analysis of the Polity data indicates that more countries are democratic than not, at least formally, that doesn't mean people are happy with democracy in action.

In a Pew Research Center survey of 27 countries conducted last year, a global median of 51% said they were dissatisfied with how democracy is working in their country, while 45% said they were satisfied. (All but one of the 27 countries in the Center's survey are considered democratic by the Polity IV methodology; the exception is Russia, which is in the "mixed" category.)

Of the countries surveyed, Sweden and the Philippines were among those with the highest levels of popular satisfaction with democracy: 69% in each nation said they were satisfied. (Indonesia, South Korea and the Netherlands weren't far behind.) At the other end, people in Mexico, Greece, Brazil and Spain expressed the most dissatisfaction with the state of democracy in their countries.

Print Citations

CMS: DeSilver, Drew. "Despite Global Concerns about Democracy, More Than Half of Countries Are Democratic." In *The Reference Shelf: Democracy Evolving,* edited by Micah L. Issitt, 117-119. Amenia, NY: Grey House Publishing, 2019.

MLA: DeSilver, Drew. "Despite Global Concerns about Democracy, More Than Half of Countries Are Democratic." *The Reference Shelf: Democracy Evolving,* edited by Micah L. Issitt, Grey Housing Publishing, 2019, pp. 117-119.

APA: DeSilver, D. (2019). Despite global concerns about democracy, more than half of countries are democratic. In Micah L. Issitt (Ed.), *The reference shelf: Democracy evolving* (pp. 117-119). Amenia, NY: Grey Housing Publishing.

Democracy Is More Fragile Than Many of Us Realized, but Don't Believe That It Is Doomed

By Andrew Rawnsley
The Guardian, January 20, 2019

Nothing ages so badly as visions of the future. When the fall of the Berlin Wall was followed by the implosion of the Soviet Union, Francis Fukuyama celebrated by publishing his bestseller, *The End of History and the Last Man*. The book argued that, with the demise of its main ideological competitor, the world would belong to liberal democracy. He has been much mocked since for failing to foresee that democracy would face the emergence of fresh threats and the resurgence of old foes in new guises in the shape of nationalism, religious extremism, autocratic capitalism, unaccountable tech titans, cyber warfare and even, in the case of North Korea, legacy Stalinism. But fair's fair. For a while at least, his thesis was true.

The end of the Cold War accelerated what is sometimes referred to as "the third wave" of democratisation in the late 20th century. The peoples of Eastern Europe were liberated to choose their own governments. African presidents-for-life were sent into retirement. Much of Latin America, once a grisly tableau of coups, insurgencies, juntas and death squads, embraced the tenets of democracy. India was no longer a shining exception to autocracy in developing Asia, as more of the world's most populous continent followed the democratic path. By the turn of the century, more than 100 countries could be reasonably classified as democracies, albeit often flawed ones. A hundred years before, you could barely find 10 democracies on the world map. If your definition of democracy includes, as really it ought to, women having the vote, then there was New Zealand by 1900 and some bits of Australia and that was it.

Democracy won the 20th century. The hubristic mistake was to think that this trend was so powerful that it could not be reversed. The size of that error is illustrated by the latest report from Freedom House, a non-partisan thinktank that conducts an annual audit of global freedom. The fundamentals of democracy, particularly regular and honest elections, a free media, the rule of law and the rights of minorities, are under attack around the world. Last year was the 12th consecutive one in which the number of countries becoming more free were outnumbered by those becoming less so. The report's authors conclude that "democracy is in crisis".

Does the evidence justify this alarming assessment? Some autocratic brutes have been given the boot, among them Robert Mugabe, whose removal at least gives the possibility of a better future for Zimbabwe. Many countries remain robustly democratic. Britons may feel a squeak of patriotic pride that Freedom House awards a high 94 points to our country. You have to be Scandinavian to achieve the maximum 100.

It is hard, though, to disagree that the big picture is a negative one. From Venezuela to the Philippines, more countries have become less free. And many of those countries that remain democracies are becoming more dysfunctional. The charnel house that is Syria is a daily reminder that the hopes associated with the Arab spring have crumbled into the dust. Tunisia, democracy's lonely outpost in the Arab world, is now very troubled. Closer to home, there is the slide into autocratic rule in Turkey and creeping authoritarianism in Poland and Hungary, countries that had been presumed to be permanent gains for liberal democracy. The danger here is not so much the old spectre of tanks on the streets. The dismantling of freedom begins with attacks on what some call "the soft guard rails" of democracy: unfettered media, an independent judiciary, a basic level of respect for political opponents. Freedom is not devoured in one gulp, but in a series of bite-size chunks.

Political scientists are conducting a lively argument about how worried we should be and what has caused this global retreat, but I think we can pick out some clear drivers of what has gone wrong. Start with the democratic victors of the Cold War. Their cohesion and confidence are being corroded by economic pressures, social inequalities, rebellions against the consequences of globalisation and a resurgence of

> **Division and disarray among democracies has encouraged the pursuit of an aggressively anti-freedom agenda by the major autocracies, China and Russia.**

nationalism and regionalism. Populists of left and right have exploited voter anger to gain support and parliamentary seats across Europe. The result is that they have got into power in some places and in others made it harder for mainstream parties to form viable coalitions, as in the Netherlands and Germany. This wave has not yet broken. Ahead of Italy's elections in March, populists of left and right lead the polls and have cornered two thirds of the electorate.

Populists have profited at the ballot box by telling voters that democracy is a sham or a scam rigged in favour of outsiders or an elite or both. The populist prescriptions are nearly always snake oil, but their diagnosis has resonance with many voters because the economic discontents are real. It is no coincidence, as the old Marxists liked to say, that western democracy has come under so much stress since the Great Crash of 2008 and the protracted squeeze on living standards that has followed it.

In western countries that previously promoted liberal values, there is what Human Rights Watch calls a "frontal assault on the values of inclusivity, tolerance and respect". America is mesmerised by Trump. Britain is obsessed with Brexit.

Germany struggles to put together a government. All have become fractiously in-
ward looking. This has bloody consequences for the rest of the world, by helping to
allow mass atrocities in Myanmar, South Sudan, Syria and Yemen to continue with
near impunity.

The United States has shrunk from its traditional role as exemplar of democracy
and global champion of it. America was always extremely imperfect in this role, but
its postwar leaders at least paid lip service to the idea that the shining city on the
hill should be a beacon of liberty. The Oval Office is occupied by a president who
has spent his first year in office trashing democratic norms at home while expressing no sense of responsibility to be an advocate for universal human rights. He has
triggered a plunge in international respect for American leadership to a record low.
The United States has often in the past been an enabler of undemocratic regimes,
but never before has it had a president who expresses so much open admiration for
authoritarians in the Kremlin and elsewhere, and so much undisguised contempt
for his country's traditional allies among the other democracies.

Division and disarray among democracies has encouraged the pursuit of an ag-
gressively anti-freedom agenda by the major autocracies, China and Russia. During
the optimism of the third wave, it was presumed that democracy had a world-win-
ning formula. The more prosperous countries became, the more they would want
to be free; the more free they were, the more prosperous they would become. The
belief that a richer China ought to become a more liberal China is not shared by
President Xi Jinping. He is intensifying repression at home and promoting the Chinese model of autocratic capitalism as a superior recipe for stability and prosperity.
It was Xi's recent boast that China is "blazing a trail" for developing countries to
emulate. China's autocrats blaze while the democracies fiddle.

A s is their way, political scientists have seen a disturbing phenomenon and
given it geeky labels. Some call it "democratic deconsolidation". Others go for "democratic recession". I prefer "recession", because at least that description implies a
seed of hope that this trend does not have to be permanent. Recessions can and
usually do come to an end.

Reading the recent flurry of reports about the endangerment of liberty around
the world, you could be driven to the despairing conclusion that democracy is dying.
That fatalism would be as large an error as the assumption that democracy would be
everywhere and permanently triumphant. Democracy has a lot going for it, not least
that it is a better form of government than any other type that the human race has
yet managed to design. Millions of South Koreans are not trying to flee to the north.
There was something both bizarre and fantastic about watching the White House
physician take questions from reporters about the most intimate details of the president's health on live and global television. They don't do that in dictatorships.

Democracy is not doomed. The lesson of the past decade is the subtler one
that democracy is more fragile, vulnerable and contingent than many liberals have
often complacently supposed. The arc of history is not irreversibly bent in favour of

freedom. The case for it has to be renewed and reinvigorated for each generation. The biggest mistake we make about democracy is to take it for granted.

Print Citations

CMS: Rawnsley, Andrew. "Democracy Is More Fragile Than Many of Us Realized, but Don't Believe That It Is Doomed." In *The Reference Shelf: Democracy Evolving,* edited by Micah L. Issitt, 120-123. Amenia, NY: Grey House Publishing, 2019.

MLA: Rawnsley, Andrew. "Democracy Is More Fragile Than Many of Us Realized, but Don't Believe That It Is Doomed." *The Reference Shelf: Democracy Evolving,* edited by Micah L. Issitt, Grey Housing Publishing, 2019, pp. 120-123.

APA: Rawnsley, A. (2019). Democracy is more fragile than many of us realized, but don't believe that it is doomed. In Micah L. Issitt (Ed.), *The reference shelf: Democracy evolving* (pp. 120-123). Amenia, NY: Grey Housing Publishing.

Poland's Nationalism Threatens Europe's Values, and Cohesion

By Steven Erlanger and Marc Santora
The New York Times, February 20, 2019

SNIADOWO, Poland—The young mayor of this small town deep in eastern Poland is extremely proud of its new Italian fire engine, which sits, resplendent, next to a Soviet-era one. Nearby, the head of the elementary school shows off new classrooms and a new gymnasium, complete with an electronic scoreboard.

All of this—plus roads, solar panels, and improved water purification and sewer systems, as well as support to dairy farmers—has largely been paid for by the European Union, which finances nearly 60 percent of Poland's public investment.

With such largess, one would hardly think that Poland is in a kind of war with the European Union. In recent months, the nationalist government has bitten the hand that feeds it more than once.

The European Union has accused Poland of posing a grave risk to democratic values, accusing it of undermining the rule of law by packing the courts with loyalists. Western leaders have also criticized Poland's governing party for pushing virtually all critical voices off the state news media and for restricting free speech with its latest law criminalizing any suggestion that the Polish nation bore any responsibility in the Holocaust.

The tug of war has intensified as Eastern Europe becomes the incubator for a new model of "illiberal democracy" for which Hungary has laid the groundwork. But it is Poland—so large, so rich, so militarily powerful and so important geostrategically—that will define whether the European Union's long effort to integrate the former Soviet bloc succeeds or fails.

The stakes, many believe, far outweigh those of Britain's exit from the European Union, or Brexit, as the bloc faces a painful reckoning over whether, despite its efforts at discipline, it has enabled the anti-democratic drift, and what to do about it.

The growing conflict between the original Western member states of the bloc and the newer members in Central and Eastern Europe is the main threat to the cohesion and survival of the European Union. It is not a simple clash, but a multibannered one of identity, history, values, religion and interpretations of democracy and "solidarity."

"It's yes to Europe, but what Europe?" said Michal Baranowski, the director of the Warsaw office of the German Marshall Fund, noting that Poland's support for European Union membership runs as high as 80 percent but can be shallow.

The Polish government, which is dominated by the Law and Justice party, itself dominated from the back rooms by the party chief, Jaroslaw Kaczynski, seems to have its own answer to the question.

It is more than happy to take European Union economic support, but worries that Poland's share could dwindle if the member nations use the budget to pressure Poland to fall in line. The country is to get nearly 9 percent of the European Union budget for 2014 to 2020, around 85 billion euros, or $105 billion.

But the vague threats to apply the brakes to the gravy train are unlikely to push the Kaczynski government to change. It has responded to European criticism by accusing Brussels and Germany—until recently Poland's greatest ally in Europe—of dictating terms to newer members and trying to impose an elitist, secular vision. It has also positioned itself at the forefront of central and eastern European nations opposing migration quotas, saying it is acting in defense of Christian values.

The governing party has campaigned on Polish national pride and "getting up off our knees;" it has also portrayed predominantly Roman Catholic Poland, which traditionally sees itself as a victim of history, as the "Christ of nations."

After being squeezed between empires and occupied in turns by fascism and communism, Poland is ready to take its place as an equal, Mr. Kaczynski asserts, no longer relegated to serfdom or secondary status.

"The history is part of our identity, which people in other parts of the world don't understand," said Slawomir Debski, the director of the Polish Institute of International Affairs. "What is it to be a Pole? We are the nation that survived World War II and were the victims of both totalitarian systems."

This combination of Polish nationalism, religious conservatism, anti-elitism and attacks on those supposedly seeking to dictate to Poland about values and migrant quotas has made Law and Justice by far the largest party in a divided country with a disorganized political opposition.

The party has risen from almost 38 percent of the vote in the 2015 election to about 47 percent in recent opinion polls. Much of that success is attributed to its investment in the poorer countryside, and much of the money for that investment is attributed to European Union support and access to its markets and jobs.

But more than money, Law and Justice thrives on cultural and identity politics. It has contrasted a conservative, Catholic Poland and its family values with a godless, freethinking, gender-bending Western Europe.

It accuses past governments, the opposition and the urban elites of hankering after European approval and acceptance to the detriment of Polish interests.

Sniadowo district, a collection of villages northeast of Warsaw with roughly 5,500 people, reflects that support. While the pre-World War II population was about 40 percent Jewish, today it is Kaczynski country.

The area is profoundly Roman Catholic and deeply affected by its proximity to Belarus and the memories of the Soviet occupation of World War II. In 2015,

> Poland rejects a "multilevel" or "two-speed" Europe, with an inner core of eurozone states and an outer ring of lesser members.

roughly 70 percent of voters in the region supported Law and Justice.

People go to church several times a week, priests tend to give passionate, political sermons, and state and church media give a partisan version of events.

"Promoting same-sex marriage will not go down well here," said Marek Adam Komorowski, 58, a local councilman in nearby Lomza. "If you are in Europe, you can't speak against it, but it is not a norm here. Here, family means something else."

Rafal Pstragowski, the 37-year-old mayor of Sniadowo, an independent in his seventh year in office, echoed the sentiments. "Poland is a traditional Christian country and Poland respects other religions," he said, "but we want our culture to be respected, too."

"There is a fear among people that Western secularism is a threat to our traditional culture," he added. "If things in Europe keep going in the same direction, people think that the migration crisis and terrorist attacks could start here, too."

Slawomir Zgrzywa, 55, a local historian, said that Poland's long history of conflict with Russia had made it skeptical of "any sort of left-wing or liberal politics," and had enhanced the standing of a deeply conservative and politicized Roman Catholic priesthood.

As for the fight with the European Union over the government's control of the judiciary, that "seems abstract," said Agnieszka Walczuk, 45, the director of the town's elementary school. "The people here are poor, and they feel they have been helped by a government seen as protecting them," she said.

The recent squabble over Poland's new law about history and the Holocaust is another example of the government's offending Western European sensibilities about free speech for domestic gain. It is seen at home as an effort to protect Poland against all those angry, upset foreigners—including Jews and Western Europeans. It was telling that the opposition abstained on the vote, rather than voting against.

While firmly in favor of membership, Law and Justice has a vision of the European Union similar to the British one—a union of nation states trading freely with one another but not interfering in domestic politics or national culture.

At the same time, Poland sees an emerging vision for Europe, under the proposals of France's president, Emmanuel Macron, as reviving French-German domination of the bloc, which would leave Poland more sidelined.

In Poland's view, talk of restricting the rights of foreign workers in France is protectionist and aimed at the new member states, but wrapped in pro-European language. Poland rejects a "multilevel" or "two-speed" Europe, with an inner core of eurozone states and an outer ring of lesser members. But it sees Brussels heading that way regardless.

In general, Mr. Kaczynski's priority is domestic, "and for control of the judiciary, he's ready to pay almost any price," said Piotr Buras, the head of the Warsaw office of the European Council on Foreign Relations. "He is slowly using mostly democratic means, amassing so much power that the party's position is unassailable."

The changes, the ruling party argues, are necessary to clear out an old Communist elite, but they are "rendering the independence of the judiciary completely moot," Frans Timmermans, the vice president of the European Commission, said in December.

"The constitutionality of legislation can no longer be guaranteed," he said, because "the country's judiciary is now under the political control of the ruling majority."

The European Union has warned Poland officially, charging that Warsaw risks "a serious breach" of its commitment to shared values of liberal democracy and the rule of law, principles that all member states have sworn to uphold.

Some think that Warsaw and Brussels will compromise somehow. But that is difficult to foresee. Mr. Buras sees in Mr. Kaczynski a pessimism about the European project.

"He thinks that this E.U. is doomed to fail, and so we need to save ourselves," Mr. Buras said. "He believes that it cannot survive."

That concerns Ms. Walczuk, the school director, who remembers the paucity of her choices under Communism and worries about the future of her daughter, 16, and son, 12.

"I fear this fight with Brussels might limit my children's right to work and travel in Europe," she said. "I know my kids have no sense of not having anything, no sense that they should say something, to stand up for their rights, and this worries me."

Print Citations

CMS: Erlanger, Steven, and Marc Santora. "Poland's Nationalism Threatens Europe's Values, and Cohesion." In *The Reference Shelf: Democracy Evolving*, edited by Micah L. Issitt, 124-127. Amenia, NY: Grey House Publishing, 2019.

MLA: Erlanger, Steven, and Marc Santora. "Poland's Nationalism Threatens Europe's Values, and Cohesion." *The Reference Shelf: Democracy Evolving*, edited by Micah L. Issitt, Grey Housing Publishing, 2019, pp. 124-127.

APA: Erlanger, S., & Santora, M. (2019). Poland's nationalism threatens Europe's values, and cohesion. In Micah L. Issitt (Ed.), *The reference shelf: Democracy evolving* (pp. 124-127). Amenia, NY: Grey Housing Publishing.

5

What Do We Think of Democracy?

By US House Office of Photography, via Wikimedia.

The surprise election of Representative Alexandria Ocasio-Ccortez (D-NY) indicates the upswing in support for democratic socialism in the United States.

Attitudes and Approaches

One of the most unusual developments in twenty-first century politics is the gradual popular acceptance of alternative political ideology. In the 2010s, an increasing number of Americans have begun to express sincere interest in adopting a more socialist form of democracy, perhaps mirroring the Scandinavian countries, while there has been a similar uptick in interest in authoritarianism, mostly among those with lower education levels who identify as conservative or right-wing.[1] More generally, there is widespread skepticism about the need for democratic governance. Whether these trends represent a lasting force in American culture or are better described as a reflection of dissatisfaction with the shortfalls of the current political establishment (such as income inequality and institutionalized racism) is unclear, but the trend is pronounced enough that it may represent an important factor in America's political environment, especially as Millennials begin to assume positions of power in the government and in America's corporate institutions.

A Socialist Agenda

Democratic Representative Alexandria Ocasio-Cortez carried off an upset victory against incumbent Joe Crowley in the 2018 midterm elections relying on grassroots organizing and a focus on working-class interests and income inequality. Ocasio-Cortez became the first successful politician in decades to describe themselves as "socialist," a term few Americans understand, with negative connotations in American culture—a holdover from the long-term propagandizing against Communism during the Cold War. Since winning her election, Ocasio-Cortez has become a prime target of the Republican Party and has been characterized by them as "dangerous." President Donald Trump echoed this sentiment in a State of the Union address:

> Here, in the United States, we are alarmed by new calls to adopt socialism in our country. America was founded on liberty and independence—not government coercion, domination, and control. We are born free, and we will stay free. Tonight, we renew our resolve that American will never be a socialist country.[2]

The United States has been home to both socialist and communist political movements since the 1800s, and American adherents of these philosophies played a crucial role in the worker's rights movement that resulted in the establishment of the first federal laws against the exploitation of workers, child laborers, and women. These movements also led to the formation of the first labor unions, organizations that enable individuals working in certain fields to exercise collective influence when negotiating with management. A number of key factors have shaped American attitudes about socialism and communism. At the very beginning of the worker's rights movement, as socialists and communists were leading protests against the exploitation of the working class, business owners and allied politicians began portraying socialists and communists as dangerous radicals who posed a threat to America in an effort to prevent the imposition of laws that would force companies to make changes based on the welfare of workers.[3]

Elsewhere in the world socialism and communism became the catalyst in populist revolutions that led to the downfall of monarchic aristocracies. This occurred in Russia and China in the form of revolutionary movements that completely upended the distribution of power in those societies. This set the stage for the Cold War, an ideological conflict that began after World War II as the United States and its allies competed with the Soviet Union and China to spread their ideological vision of the world order. Given the danger of the proliferation of nuclear weapons, the United States, Russia, and China instead funded and participated in proxy wars with the goal of anchoring democratic or communist ideology in certain parts of the world. Americans were encouraged to view communism and socialism as inherently malignant political philosophies and to view those who embraced these philosophies as "anti-American," and/or "anti-freedom."

In general, communism and socialism are characterized by the belief that the government should control property and the means of production so as to ensure that the profits from a nation's collective productivity are more evenly distributed. Communism and socialism were nineteenth-century responses to aristocratic authoritarianism, in which a small number of wealthy elites dominate society. In many cases, communist and socialist governments have failed due to exploitation and greed. Russia, for instance, is not actually governed according to socialist ideals but is, instead, an authoritarian regime in which the government utilizes military and police authority to maintain an uneven distribution of wealth that includes a wealthy elite class. Socialism and communism are not inherently authoritarian, but these societies can become autocratic when a powerful political group misuses the system to limit personal freedom.

In the twenty-first century, Americans who promote socialism generally embrace what is called "democratic socialism," which is similar to the type of government utilized in Sweden and elsewhere in Scandinavia. Democratic socialism reflects the belief that the primary purpose of the government is to actively intervene to improve the lives of the people. Democratic socialists generally favor policies similar to the "New Deal" of the 1930s, a series of proactive governmental policies designed to prevent a repetition of the Great Depression. In the twenty-first century, Democratic socialists like Bernie Sanders and Ocasio-Cortez support such socialist policies as free public higher education, universal or at least extremely low-cost healthcare systems, federal job creation and training programs, and graduated taxation based on wealth. Democratic socialists also tend to favor an expansion of federal and state welfare systems designed to assist those living in poverty. The Democratic Socialists of America is the most prominent political organization advocating for Scandinavian-style socialist policies for America.[4]

Supporters of democratic socialism often point to the Scandinavian countries, like Sweden and Finland, where socialist policies have been utilized for decades to prevent poverty and to prohibit economic exploitation by a wealthy elite. Critics argue that such societies incur extremely high tax burdens; supporters argue that the reduction in cost for health care and education offsets increased taxation. Critics argue that governments cannot be trusted to act in the interest of the people and that socialist policies invite authoritarianism or exploitation. Supporters argue that corporations and the wealthy, who typically wield outsized influence in free-market capitalist societies, also cannot be trusted to act in the interest of the public.[5]

Some claim that socialism is incompatible with American values or with democracy, however. The United States has "socialized" key societal systems, like public education and publicly funded law enforcement, and these have been important in expanding the benefits of education and the protection of the law to a greater share of the American people. The primary opposition to socialism is more economic than ideological, as the establishment of democratic socialist policies would upend the economic hierarchy in industries such as healthcare and banking. Representatives of these industries and allied politicians have therefore campaigned against public interest in democratic socialism and have portrayed the philosophy as inherently dangerous.

Democratic Malaise

One of the greatest challenges faced by any democratic government is to inspire and encourage public participation in the political process and to engender faith and trust in the political system. For decades, the percentage of Americans who express full trust in America's government and political system has been falling. In 1960, during the conservative Dwight Eisenhower administration, an average of 73 percent of Americans believed that they could trust their government to protect their interests all or most of the time. By 2019, this percentage had fallen to 17 percent. The percentage of Americans who feel they can trust the government to "do what is right" almost all the time sits at only 3 percent of the population.[6] The reasons for the loss of government trust are complex, but the phenomenon is closely related to America's long-lasting struggle with income inequality, identity politics, and to the increasing polarization of America's political environment.

The partisan divide between those identifying as right wing or conservative and those identifying as left-wing or progressive has been intensifying over the past two decades, reaching a historic level in the 2010s.[7] The increasingly divisive political environment has become more so since President Donald Trump and his administration have demonstrated an aversion to negotiation and compromise and has embraced policies that appeal to minority interest groups but do not reflect the views of the majority of Americans. Another sign of increasing dissatisfaction with America's democracy is the apathy of Americans with regard to participation in the political process. As of 2019, the United States has fallen behind most of the world's developed nations in terms of voter interest and participation; only 56 percent of eligible voters cast votes in the 2016 election, placing the United States 26th out of 32 developed nations in which voting patterns were analyzed by the Organization for Economic Cooperation and Development (OECD).[8] Lack of voter participation is related to America's increasing partisanship and the feeling of being unrepresented by one's government . . . many Americans feel that their vote doesn't count. The erosion of America's political system also impacts citizen participation. For instance, a series of leaked documents from North Carolina in May of 2019 revealed that the North Carolina Republican party had purposefully redistricted voting districts to limit the weight of Democratic votes and concentrate Republican voters in key districts. Such activities erode the legitimacy of the democratic process and reinforce the perception that voting is meaningless to the outcome of state or national elections.[9]

Voter apathy is especially pronounced among the Millennial generation (1980-1999), as are many other measures of dissatisfaction with America's current political environment. Studies show that, among Millennials, the view that democracy is no longer necessary to America's future has gained surprising traction. Millennials are far more likely than the population as a whole to be critical of America's democratic system, to look favorably on radical changes like socialist or authoritarian changes to U.S. politics, and to express the sense that individual participation in the process is ineffective.

As the current generation in power expires or retires, dramatic changes to America's political system may come to pass. As of 2019, the American government is still dominated by members of the Baby Boomer generation (1946–1964). Members of Generation X (1965–1979) are slowly taking the place of the Baby Boomers within the government. Following them are members of the Millennials (1980–1999), and then Generation Z (or the Centennials, late 1990s–2010s). As power is transferred between generations, the direction of America's government and of the evolution of society necessarily changes. The discord among the Millennials is due in part to the fact that they are living in a world dominated by views and ideologies they consider outmoded and outdated. Demographers and social scientists have noted differences between Millennial views of society and those of previous generations. Millennials may alter the status quo in significant ways, but this will depend largely on the degree to which they retain or abandon their tendency toward more radical solutions to the perennial problems that plague American society.

Works Used

Desilver, Drew. "U.S. Trails Most Developed Countries in Voter Turnout." *Pew Research*. May 21, 2018. Retrieved from https://www.pewresearch.org/fact-tank/2018/05/21/u-s-voter-turnout-trails-most-developed-countries/.

Haltiwanger, John. "Here's the Difference between a 'Socialist' and a 'Democratic Socialist'." *Business Insider*. Feb 25, 2019. Retrieved from https://www.businessinsider.com/difference-between-socialist-and-democratic-socialist-2018-6.

Lipset, Seymour Martin and Gary Marks. *It Didn't Happen Here: Why Socialism Failed in the United States*. New York: W.W. Norton & Company, 2000.

"Public Trust in Government: 1958-2019." *Pew Research Center*. Apr 11, 2019. Retrieved from https://www.people-press.org/2019/04/11/public-trust-in-government-1958-2019/.

Stern, Mark Joseph. "The New Trove of Secret Gerrymandering Files Will Be a Nightmare for the GOP." *Slate*. May 31, 2019. Retrieved from https://slate.com/news-and-politics/2019/05/thomas-hofeller-secret-gerrymandering-files-north-carolina.html.

Taylor, Jessica. "Republicans and Democrats Don't Agree, or Like Each Other—And It's Worse Than Ever." *NPR*. Oct 5, 2017. Retrieved from https://www.npr.org/2017/10/05/555685136/republicans-and-democrats-dont-agree-dont-like-each-other-and-its-worst-than-eve.

Waxman, Olivia B. "Socialism Was Once America's Political Taboo: Now, Democratic Socialism Is a Viable Platform. Here's What to Know." *Time*. Oct 24, 2018. Retrieved from http://time.com/5422714/what-is-democratic-socialism/.

"Who We Are & What We Do." *DSA*. Democratic Socialists of America. Retrieved from https://www.dsausa.org.

Wike, Richard, Simmons, Katie, Stokes, Bruce, and Janell Fetterolf. "Democracy Widely Supported, Little Backing for Rule by Strong Leader or Military." *Pew Research Center*. Oct 16, 2017. Retrieved from https://www.pewresearch.org/global/2017/10/16/democracy-widely-supported-little-backing-for-rule-by-strong-leader-or-military/.

Notes

1. Wike, Simmons, Stokes, and Fetterolf, "Democracy Widely Supported, Little Backing for Rule by Stong Leader or Military."
2. Haltiwanger, "Here's the Difference between a 'Socialist' and a 'Democratic Socialist'."
3. Lipset and Marks, *It Didn't Happen Here: Why Socialism Failed in the United States*.
4. "Who We Are & What We Do," *DSA*.
5. Waxman, "Socialism Was Once America's Political Taboo: Now, Democratic Socialism Is a Viable Platform. Here's What to Know."
6. "Public Trust in Government: 1958-2019," *Pew Research Center*.
7. Taylor, "Republicans and Democrats Don't Agree, or Like Each Other—And It's Worse Than Ever."
8. Desilver, "U.S. Trails Most Developed Countries in Voter Turnout."
9. Stern, "The New Trove of Secret Gerrymandering Files Will Be a Nightmare for the GOP."

The Public, the Political System and American Democracy

Pew Research Center, April 26, 2018

At a time of growing stress on democracy around the world, Americans generally agree on democratic ideals and values that are important for the United States. But for the most part, they see the country falling well short in living up to these ideals, according to a new study of opinion on the strengths and weaknesses of key aspects of American democracy and the political system.

The public's criticisms of the political system run the gamut, from a failure to hold elected officials accountable to a lack of transparency in government. And just a third say the phrase "people agree on basic facts even if they disagree politically" describes this country well today.

The perceived shortcomings encompass some of the core elements of American democracy. An overwhelming share of the public (84%) says it is very important that "the rights and freedoms of all people are respected." Yet just 47% say this describes the country very or somewhat well; slightly more (53%) say it does not.

Despite these criticisms, most Americans say democracy is working well in the United States—though relatively few say it is working *very* well. At the same time, there is broad support for making sweeping changes to the political system: 61% say "significant changes" are needed in the fundamental "design and structure" of American government to make it work for current times.

The public sends mixed signals about *how* the American political system should be changed, and no proposals attract bipartisan support. Yet in views of how many of the specific aspects of the political system are working, both Republicans and Democrats express dissatisfaction.

To be sure, there are some positives. A sizable majority of Americans (74%) say the military leadership in the U.S. does not publicly support one party over another, and nearly as many (73%) say the phrase "people are free to peacefully protest" describes this country very or somewhat well.

In general, however, there is a striking mismatch between the public's goals for American democracy and its views of whether they are being fulfilled. On 23 specific measures assessing democracy, the political system and elections in the United States—each widely regarded by the public as very important—there are only eight on which majorities say the country is doing even somewhat well.

The new survey of the public's views of democracy and the political system by

Pew Research Center was conducted online Jan. 29-Feb. 13 among 4,656 adults. It was supplemented by a survey conducted March 7-14 among 1,466 adults on landlines and cellphones.

Among the major findings:

Mixed views of structural changes in the political system. The surveys examine several possible changes to representative democracy in the United States. Most Americans reject the idea of amending the Constitution to give states with larger populations more seats in the U.S. Senate, and there is little support for expanding the size of the House of Representatives. As in the past, however, a majority (55%) supports changing the way presidents are elected so that the candidate who receives the most total votes nationwide—rather than a majority in the Electoral College—wins the presidency.

A majority says Trump lacks respect for democratic institutions. Fewer than half of Americans (45%) say Donald Trump has a great deal or fair amount of respect for the country's democratic institutions and traditions, while 54% say he has not too much respect or no respect. These views are deeply split along partisan and ideological lines. Most conservative Republicans (55%) say Trump has a "great deal" of respect for democratic institutions; most liberal Democrats (60%) say he has no respect "at all" for these traditions and institutions.

Government and politics seen as working better locally than nationally. Far more Americans have a favorable opinion of their local government (67%) than of the federal government (35%). In addition, there is substantial satisfaction with the quality of candidates running for Congress and local elections in recent elections. That stands in contrast with views of the recent presidential candidates; just 41% say the quality of presidential candidates in recent elections has been good.

Few say tone of political debate is "respectful." Just a quarter of Americans say "the tone of debate among political leaders is respectful" is a statement that describes the country well. However, the public is more divided in general views about tone and discourse: 55% say too many people are "easily offended" over the language others use; 45% say people need to be more careful in using language "to avoid offending" others.

Americans don't spare themselves from criticism. In addressing the shortcomings of the political system, Americans do not spare themselves from criticism: Just 39% say "voters are knowledgeable about candidates and issues" describes the country very or somewhat well. In addition, a 56% majority say they have little or no confidence in the political wisdom of the American people. However, that is less negative than in early 2016, when 64% had little or no confidence. Since the presidential election, Republicans have become more confident in people's political wisdom.

Cynicism about money and politics. Most Americans think that those who donate a lot of money to elected officials have more political influence than others. An overwhelming majority (77%) supports limits on the amount of money individuals and organizations can spend on political campaigns and issues. And nearly two-thirds of Americans (65%) say new laws could be effective in reducing the role of money in politics.

Varying views of obligations of good citizenship. Large majorities say it is very important to vote, pay taxes and always follow the law in order to be a good citizen. Half of Americans say it is very important to know the Pledge of Allegiance, while 45% say it is very important to protest government actions a person believes is wrong. Just 36% say displaying the American flag is very important to being a good citizen.

Most are aware of basic facts about political system and democracy. Overwhelming shares correctly identify the constitutional right guaranteed by the First Amendment to the Constitution and know the role of the Electoral College. A narrower majority knows how a tied vote is broken in the Senate, while fewer than half know the number of votes needed to break a Senate filibuster.

Democracy Seen as Working Well, but Most Say "Significant Changes" Are Needed

In general terms, most Americans think U.S. democracy is working at least somewhat well. Yet a 61% majority says "significant changes" are needed in the fundamental "design and structure" of American government to make it work in current times. When asked to compare the U.S. political system with those of other developed nations, fewer than half rate it "above average" or "best in the world."

Overall, nearly six-in-ten Americans (58%) say democracy in the United States is working very or somewhat well, though just 18% say it is working *very* well. Four-in-ten say it is working not too well or not at all well.

Republicans have more positive views of the way democracy is working than do Democrats: 72% of Republicans and Republican-leaning independents say democracy in the U.S. is working at least somewhat well, though only 30% say it is working very well. Among Democrats and Democratic leaners, 48% say democracy works at least somewhat well, with just 7% saying it is working very well.

More Democrats than Republicans say significant changes are needed in the design and structure of government. By more than two-to-one (68% to 31%), Democrats say significant changes are needed. Republicans are evenly divided: 50% say significant changes are needed in the

> **61% say "significant changes" are needed in the fundamental "design and structure" of American government to make it work for current times.**

structure of government, while 49% say the current structure serves the country well and does not need significant changes.

The public has mixed evaluations of the nation's political system compared with those of other developed countries. About four-in-ten say the U.S. political system is the best in the world (15%) or above average (26%); most say it is average (28%) or below average (29%), when compared with other developed nations. Several other national institutions and aspects of life in the U.S—including the military, standard of living and scientific achievements—are more highly rated than the political system.

Republicans are about twice as likely as Democrats to say the U.S. political system is best in the world or above average (58% vs. 27%). As recently as four years ago, there were no partisan differences in these opinions.

Bipartisan Criticism of Political System in a Number of Areas

Majorities in both parties say "people are free to peacefully protest" describes the U.S. well. And there is bipartisan sentiment that the military leadership in the U.S. does not publicly favor one party over another.

In most cases, however, partisans differ on how well the country lives up to democratic ideals—or majorities in both parties say it is falling short.

Some of the most pronounced partisan differences are in views of equal opportunity in the U.S. and whether the rights and freedoms of all people are respected.

Republicans are twice as likely as Democrats to say "everyone has an equal opportunity to succeed" describes the United States very or somewhat well (74% vs. 37%).

A majority of Republicans (60%) say the rights and freedoms of all people are respected in the United States, compared with just 38% of Democrats.

And while only about half of Republicans (49%) say the country does well in respecting "the views of people who are not in the majority on issues," even fewer Democrats (34%) say this.

No more than about a third in either party say elected officials who engage in misconduct face serious consequences or that government "conducts its work openly and transparently." Comparably small shares in both parties (28% of Republicans, 25% of Democrats) say the following sentence describes the country well: "People who give a lot of money to elected officials *do not* have more political influence than other people."

Fewer than half in both parties also say news organizations do not favor one political party, though Democrats are more likely than Republicans to say this describes the country well (38% vs. 18%). There also is skepticism in both parties about the political independence of judges. Nearly half of Democrats (46%) and 38% of Republicans say judges are not influenced by political parties.

Partisan Gaps in Opinions about Many Aspects of U.S. Elections

For the most part, Democrats and Republicans agree about the importance of many principles regarding elections in the U.S.

Overwhelming shares in both parties say it is very important that elections are free from tampering (91% of Republicans, 88% of Democrats say this) and that voters are knowledgeable about candidates and issues (78% in both parties).

But there are some notable differences: Republicans are almost 30 percentage points more likely than Democrats to say it is very important that "no ineligible voters are permitted to vote" (83% of Republicans vs. 55% of Democrats).

And while majorities in both parties say high turnout in presidential elections is very important, more Democrats (76%) than Republicans (64%) prioritize high voter turnout.

The differences are even starker in evaluations of how well the country is doing in fulfilling many of these objectives. Republicans are more likely than Democrats to say that "no *eligible* voters are prevented from voting" describes elections in the U.S. very or somewhat well (80% vs. 56%). By contrast, more Democrats (76%) than Republicans (42%) say "no *ineligible* voters are permitted to vote" describes elections well.

Democrats—particularly politically engaged Democrats—are critical of the process for determining congressional districts. A majority of Republicans (63%) say the way congressional voting districts are determined is fair and reasonable compared with just 39% of Democrats; among Democrats who are highly politically engaged, just 29% say the process is fair.

And fewer Democrats than Republicans consider voter turnout for elections in the U.S.—both presidential and—to be "high." Nearly three-quarters of Republicans (73%) say "there is high voter turnout in presidential elections" describes elections well, compared with only about half of Democrats (52%).

Still, there are a few points of relative partisan agreement: Majorities in both parties (62% of Republicans, 55% of Democrats) say "elections are free from tampering." And Republicans and Democrats are about equally skeptical about whether voters are knowledgeable about candidates and issues (40% of Republicans, 38% of Democrats).

Print Citations

CMS: "The Public, the Political System, and American Democracy." In *The Reference Shelf: Democracy Evolving,* edited by Micah L. Issitt, 137-141. Amenia, NY: Grey House Publishing, 2019.

MLA: "The Public, the Political System, and American Democracy." *The Reference Shelf: Democracy Evolving,* edited by Micah L. Issitt, Grey Housing Publishing, 2019, pp. 137-141.

APA: Pew Research Center. (2019). The public, the political system, and American democracy. In Micah L. Issitt (Ed.), *The reference shelf: Democracy evolving* (pp. 137-141). Amenia, NY: Grey Housing Publishing.

20 of America's Top Political Scientists Gathered to Discuss Our Democracy: They're Scared

By Sean Illing
Vox, October 13, 2017

Is American democracy in decline? Should we be worried?

On October 6, some of America's top political scientists gathered at Yale University to answer these questions. And nearly everyone agreed: American democracy is eroding on multiple fronts—socially, culturally, and economically.

The scholars pointed to breakdowns in social cohesion (meaning citizens are more fragmented than ever), the rise of tribalism, the erosion of democratic norms such as a commitment to rule of law, and a loss of faith in the electoral and economic systems as clear signs of democratic erosion.

No one believed the end is nigh, or that it's too late to solve America's many problems. Scholars said that America's institutions are where democracy has proven most resilient. So far at least, our system of checks and balances is working—the courts are checking the executive branch, the press remains free and vibrant, and Congress is (mostly) fulfilling its role as an equal branch.

But there was a sense that the alarm bells are ringing.

Yascha Mounk, a lecturer in government at Harvard University, summed it up well: "If current trends continue for another 20 or 30 years, democracy will be toast."

"Democracies Don't Fall Apart—They're Taken Apart"

Nancy Bermeo, a politics professor at Princeton and Harvard, began her talk with a jarring reminder: Democracies don't merely collapse, as that "implies a process devoid of will." Democracies die because of deliberate decisions made by human beings.

Usually, it's because the people in power take democratic institutions for granted. They become disconnected from the citizenry. They develop interests separate and apart from the voters. They push policies that benefit themselves and harm the broader population. Do that long enough, Bermeo says, and you'll cultivate an angry, divided society that pulls apart at the seams.

So how might this look in America?

Adam Przeworski, a democratic theorist at New York University, suggested that democratic erosion in America begins with a breakdown in what he calls the "class compromise." His point is that democracies thrive so long as people believe they can improve their lot in life. This basic belief has been "an essential ingredient of Western civilization during the past 200 years," he said.

But fewer and fewer Americans believe this is true. Due to wage stagnation, growing inequalities, automation, and a shrinking labor market, millions of Americans are deeply pessimistic about the future: 64 percent of people in Europe believe their children will be worse off than they were; the number is 60 percent in America.

That pessimism is grounded in economic reality. In 1970, 90 percent of 30-year-olds in America were better off than their parents at the same age. In 2010, only 50 percent were. Numbers like this cause people to lose faith in the system. What you get is a spike in extremism and a retreat from the political center. That leads to declines in voter turnout and, consequently, more opportunities for fringe parties and candidates.

Political polarization is an obvious problem, but researchers like Przeworski suggest something more profound is going on. Political theorists like to talk about the "social compact," which is basically an implicit agreement among members of society to participate in a system that benefits everyone.

Well, that only works if the system actually delivers on its promises. If it fails to do so, if it leads enough people to conclude that the alternative is less scary than the status quo, the system will implode from within.

Is that happening here? Neither Przeworski nor anyone else went quite that far. But we know there's a growing disconnect between productivity (how hard people work) and compensation (how much they're paid for that work). At the same time, we've seen a spike in racial animus, particularly on the right. It seems likely there's a connection here.

Przeworski believes that American democracy isn't collapsing so much as deteriorating. "Our divisions are not merely political but have deep roots in society," he argues. The system has become too rigged and too unfair, and most people have no real faith in it.

Where does that leave us? Nowhere good, Przeworski says. The best he could say is that "our current crisis will continue for the foreseeable future."

"The Soft Guardrails of Democracy" Are Eroding

We've heard a lot of chatter recently about the importance of democratic norms. These are the unwritten rules and the conventions that undergird a democracy—things like commitment to rule of law, to a free press, to the separation of powers, to the basic liberties of speech, assembly, religion, and property.

Daniel Ziblatt, a politics professor at Harvard, called these norms "the soft guardrails of democracy." Dying democracies, he argued, are always preceded by the breaking of these unwritten rules.

Research conducted by Bright Line Watch, the group that organized the Yale conference, shows that Americans are not as committed to these norms as you might expect.

It's not that Americans don't believe in democratic ideals or principles; it's that our beliefs scale with our partisan loyalties. *Vox*'s Ezra Klein explained it well in a recent column:

People's opinions on democracy lie downstream from their partisan identity. If it had been Trump's voters who had seen the Electoral College, gerrymandering, and Russia turn against them, then it would be Trump's voters vibrating with outrage over the violation of key principles of American democracy.

Hypocrisy aside, the reaction of nearly half the country to Russia's meddling says a lot about our attachment to core democratic values like free and fair elections.

Another startling finding is that many Americans are open to "alternatives" to democracy. In 1995, for example, one in 16 Americans supported Army rule; in 2014, that number increased to one in six. According to another survey cited at the conference, 18 percent of Americans think a military-led government is a "fairly good" idea.

But there's more.

Ziblatt identified what he calls two "master norms." The first is mutual toleration—whether we "accept the basic legitimacy of our opponents." The second is institutional forbearance—whether politicians responsibly wield the power of the institutions they're elected to control.

As for mutual toleration, America is failing abysmally (more on this below). We're hardly better on the institutional forbearance front.

Most obviously, there's Donald Trump, who has dispensed with one democratic norm after another. He's fired an FBI director in order to undercut an investigation into his campaign's possible collusion with Moscow; staffed his White House with family members; regularly attacked the free press; and refused to divest himself of his business interests.

The Republican Party, with few exceptions, has tolerated these violations in the hope that they might advance their agenda. But it's about a lot more than Republicans capitulating to Trump.

Ziblatt points to the GOP's unprecedented blocking of President Obama's Supreme Court nominee, Judge Merrick Garland, in 2016 as an example of institutional recklessness. In 2013, Senate Democrats took a similarly dramatic step by eliminating filibusters for most presidential nominations. That same year, House Republicans endangered the nation's credit rating and shut down the government over Obamacare.

There are countless other encroachments one could cite, but the point is clear enough: American democracy is increasingly less anchored by norms and traditions—and history suggests that's a sign of democratic decay.

"We Don't Trust Each Other"

Timur Kuran, a professor of economics and politics at Duke University, argued that the real danger we face isn't that we no longer trust the government but that we no longer trust each other.

Kuran calls it the problem of "intolerant communities,"

> **The social compact is broken. So now we're left to stew in our racial and cultural resentments.**

and he says there are two such communities in America today: "identitarian" activists concerned with issues like racial/gender equality, and the "nativist" coalition, people suspicious of immigration and cultural change.

Each of these communities defines itself in terms of its opposition to the other. They live in different worlds, desire different things, and share almost nothing in common. There is no real basis for agreement and thus no reason to communicate.

The practical consequence of this is a politics marred by tribalism. Worse, because the fault lines run so deep, every political contest becomes an intractable existential drama, with each side convinced the other is not just wrong but a mortal enemy.

Consider this stat: In 1960, 5 percent of Republicans and 4 percent of Democrats objected to the idea of their children marrying across political lines. In 2010, those numbers jumped to 46 percent and 33 percent respectively. Divides like this are eating away at the American social fabric.

A 2014 Pew Research Center study reached a similar conclusion: "In both political parties, most of those who view the other party very unfavorably say that the other side's policies 'are so misguided that they threaten the nation's well-being,'" Pew reports. "Overall, 36% of Republicans and Republican leaners say that Democratic policies threaten the nation, while 27% of Democrats and Democratic leaners view GOP policies in equally stark terms."

So it's not merely that we disagree about issues; it's that we believe the other side is a grievous threat to the republic. According to Pew, the numbers above have more than doubled since 1994.

Kuran warns that autocrats tend to exploit these divisions by pushing "policies that may seem responsive to grievances but are ultimately counterproductive." Think of Donald Trump's "Muslim ban" or his insistence on building a giant wall on the southern border. Neither of these policies is likely to make a significant difference in the lives of Trump's voters, but that's not really the point.

By pandering to fears and resentments, Trump both deepens the prejudices and satisfies his base.

Donald Trump and "the Politics of Eternity"

Timothy Snyder, a Yale historian and author of the book *On Tyranny*, gave one of the more fascinating talks of the conference.

Strangely enough, Snyder talked about time as a kind of political construct. (I know that sounds weird, but bear with me.) His thesis was that you can tell a lot about the health of a democracy based on how its leaders—and citizens—orient themselves in time.

Take Trump's "Make America Great Again" slogan. The slogan itself invokes a nostalgia for a bygone era that Trump voters believe was better than today and better than their imagined future. By speaking in this way, Snyder says, Trump is rejecting conventional politics in a subtle but significant way.

Why, after all, do we strive for better policies today? Presumably it's so that our lives can be improved tomorrow. But Trump reverses this. He anchors his discourse to a mythological past, so that voters are thinking less about the future and more about what they *think* they lost.

"Trump isn't after success—he's after failure," Snyder argued. By that, he means that Trump isn't after what we'd typically consider success—passing good legislation that improves the lives of voters. Instead, Trump has defined the problems in such a way that they can't be solved. We can't be young again. We can't go backward in time. We can't relive some lost golden age. So these voters are condemned to perpetual disappointment.

The counterargument is that Trump's idealization of the past is, in its own way, an expression of a desire for a better future. If you're a Trump voter, restoring some lost version of America or revamping trade policies or rebuilding the military is a way to create a better tomorrow based on a model from the past.

For Snyder, though, that's not really the point. The point is that Trump's nostalgia is a tactic designed to distract voters from the absence of serious solutions. Trump may not be an authoritarian, Snyder warns, but this is something authoritarians typically do. They need the public to be angry, resentful, and focused on problems that can't be remedied.

Snyder calls this approach "the politics of eternity," and he believes it's a common sign of democratic backsliding because it tends to work only after society has fallen into disorder.

My (Depressing) Takeaway

Back in June, I interviewed political scientists Christopher Achen and Larry Bartels, authors of *Democracy for Realists*. They had a sobering thesis about democracy in America: Most people pay little attention to politics; when they vote, if they vote at all, they do so irrationally and for contradictory reasons.

One of the recurring themes of this conference was that Americans are becoming less committed to liberal democratic norms. But were they ever *really* committed to those norms? I'm not so sure. If Achen and Bartels are to be believed, most voters don't hold fixed principles. They have vague feelings about undefined issues, and they surrender their votes on mostly tribal grounds.

So I look at the declining faith in democratic norms and think: Most people probably never cared about abstract principles like freedom of the press or the rule of law. (We stopped teaching civics to our children long ago.) But they more or less affirmed those principles as long as they felt invested in American life.

But for all the reasons discussed above, people have gradually disengaged from the status quo. Something has cracked. Citizens have lost faith in the system. The social compact is broken. So now we're left to stew in our racial and cultural resentments, which paved the way for a demagogue like Trump.

Bottom line: I was already pretty cynical about the trajectory of American democracy when I arrived at the conference, and I left feeling justified in that cynicism. Our problems are deep and broad and stretch back decades, and the people who study democracy closest can only tell us what's wrong. They can't tell us what ought to be done.

No one can, it seems.

Print Citations

CMS: Illing, Sean. "20 of America's Top Political Scientists Gathered to Discuss Our Democracy: They're Scared." In *The Reference Shelf: Democracy Evolving*, edited by Micah L. Issitt, 142-147. Amenia, NY: Grey House Publishing, 2019.

MLA: Illing, Sean. "20 of America's Top Political Scientists Gathered to Discuss Our Democracy: They're Scared." *The Reference Shelf: Democracy Evolving*, edited by Micah L. Issitt, Grey Housing Publishing, 2019, pp. 142-147.

APA: Illing, S. (2019). 20 of America's top political scientists gathered to discuss our democracy: They're scared. In Micah L. Issitt (Ed.), *The reference shelf: Democracy evolving* (pp. 142-147). Amenia, NY: Grey Housing Publishing.

What the World Can Learn about Equality from the Nordic Model

By Geoffrey M. Hodgson

The Conversation, July 30, 2018

Rising inequality is one of the biggest social and economic issues of our time. It is linked to poorer economic growth and fosters social discontent and unrest. So, given that the five Nordic countries—Denmark, Finland, Iceland, Norway and Sweden—are some of the world's most equal on a number of measures, it makes sense to look to them for lessons in how to build a more equal society.

The Nordic countries are all social-democratic countries with mixed economies. They are not socialist in the classical sense—they are driven by financial markets rather than by central plans, although the state does play a strategic role in the economy. They have systems of law that protect personal and corporate property and help to enforce contracts. They are democracies with checks, balances and countervailing powers.

Nordic countries show that major egalitarian reforms and substantial welfare states are possible within prosperous capitalist countries that are highly engaged in global markets. But their success undermines the view that the most ideal capitalist economy is one where markets are unrestrained. They also suggest that humane and equal outcomes are possible within capitalism, while full-blooded socialism has always, in practice, led to disaster.

The Nordic countries are among the most equal in terms of distribution of income. Using the Gini coefficient measure of income inequality (where 1 represents complete inequality and 0 represents complete equality) OECD data gives the US a score of 0.39 and the UK a slightly more equal score of 0.35—both above the OECD average of 0.31. The five Nordic countries, meanwhile, ranged from 0.25 (Iceland—the most equal) to 0.28 (Sweden).

The relative standing of the Nordic countries in terms of their distributions of wealth is not so egalitarian, however. Data show that Sweden has higher wealth inequality than France, Germany, Japan and the UK, but lower wealth inequality than the US. Norway is more equal, with wealth inequality exceeding Japan but lower than France, Germany, UK and US.

Nonetheless, the Nordic countries score very highly in terms of major welfare and development indicators. Norway and Denmark rank first and fifth in the United Nations Human Development Index. Denmark, Finland, Norway and Sweden have been among the six least corrupt countries in the world, according to the corruption perceptions index produced by Transparency International. By the same measure, the UK ranks tenth, Iceland 14th and the US 18th.

> **Exporting the Nordic model would create major challenges of assimilation, integration, trust-enhancement, consensus-building and institution-formation.**

The four largest Nordic countries have taken up the top four positions in global indices of press freedom. Iceland, Norway and Finland took the top three positions in a global index of gender equality, with Sweden in fifth place, Denmark in 14th place and the US in 49th.

Suicide rates in Denmark and Norway are lower than the world average. In Denmark, Iceland and Norway the suicide rates are lower than in the US, France and Japan. The suicide rate in Sweden is about the same as in the US, but in Finland it is higher. Norway was ranked as the happiest country in the world in 2017, followed immediately by Denmark and Iceland. By the same happiness index, Finland ranks sixth, Sweden tenth and the US 15th.

In terms of economic output (GDP) per capita, Norway is 3% above the US, while Iceland, Denmark, Sweden and Finland are respectively 11%, 14%, 14% and 25% below the US. This is a mixed, but still impressive, performance. Every Nordic country's per capita GDP is higher than the UK, France and Japan.

Special Conditions?

Clearly, the Nordic countries have achieved very high levels of welfare and well-being, alongside levels of economic output that compare well with other highly developed countries. They result from relatively high levels of social solidarity and taxation, alongside a political and economic system that preserves enterprise, economic autonomy and aspiration.

Yet the Nordic countries are small and more ethnically and culturally homogeneous than most developed countries. These special conditions have facilitated high levels of nationwide trust and cooperation—and consequently a willingness to pay higher-than-average levels of tax.

As a result, Nordic policies and institutions cannot be easily exported to other countries. Large developed countries, such as the US, UK, France and Germany, are more diverse in terms of cultures and ethnicities. Exporting the Nordic model would create major challenges of assimilation, integration, trust-enhancement, consensus-building and institution-formation. Nonetheless, it is still important to learn from it and to experiment.

Despite a prevailing global ideology in favour of markets, privatisation and macro-economic austerity, there is considerable enduring variety among capitalist countries. Furthermore some countries continue to perform much better than others on indicators of welfare and economic equality. We can learn from the Nordic mixed economies with their strong welfare provision that does not diminish the role of business. They show a way forward that is different from both statist socialism and unrestrained markets.

Print Citations

CMS: Hodgson, Geoffrey M. "What the World Can Learn about Equality from the Nordic Model." In *The Reference Shelf: Democracy Evolving,* edited by Micah L. Issitt, 148-150. Amenia, NY: Grey House Publishing, 2019.

MLA: Hodgson, Geoffrey M. "What the World Can Learn about Equality from the Nordic Model." *The Reference Shelf: Democracy Evolving,* edited by Micah L. Issitt, Grey Housing Publishing, 2019, pp. 148-150.

APA: Hodgson, G.M. (2019). What the world can learn about equality from the Nordic model. In Micah L. Issitt (Ed.), *The reference shelf: Democracy evolving* (pp. 148-150). Amenia, NY: Grey Housing Publishing.

The Nordic Democratic-Socialist Myth

By Nima Sanandaji

National Review, July 26, 2016

Although Bernie Sanders failed to win the Democratic presidential nomination, the Vermont senator's campaign did succeed in mobilizing thousands of progressive activists. Their energy and support seems closely connected to Sanders's quest to introduce a Nordic-style welfare model in the United States. As Sanders explained at the very first Democratic debate last October, "I think we should look to countries like Denmark, like Sweden and Norway, and learn from what they have accomplished for their working people."

But it's evident that the left wing of the Democratic party would also push for these ideas under a future Hillary Clinton administration. Indeed, Ezra Klein, the editor of the liberal news website *Vox*, wrote last fall that "Clinton and Sanders both want to make America look a lot more like Denmark—they both want to pass generous parental leave policies, let the government bargain down drug prices, and strengthen the social safety net."

The current president and the last Democratic president share this vision, too. In his book *Back to Work* (2011), Bill Clinton argues that Finland, Sweden, and Norway offer greater opportunities for individuals to climb the social ladder than the U.S. does. Barack Obama recently gathered the leaders of the Nordic countries in Washington, explaining that "in a world of growing economic disparities, Nordic countries have some of the least income inequality in the world—which may explain one of the reasons that they're some of the happiest people in the world."

It is not difficult to grasp the American Left's admiration for Nordic-style democratic socialism. These countries combine relatively high living standards with low poverty, long life spans, and narrow income distributions—everything the Left would like America to have. There is, however, a simple fact that seems to have escaped those who idealize Nordic-style social democracy. As I show in my forthcoming book *Debunking Utopia: Exposing the Myth of Nordic Socialism*, the social success of Nordic countries pre-dates progressive welfare-state policies.

A common misconception is that the Nordic countries became socially and economically successful by introducing universal welfare states funded by high taxes. In fact, their economic and social success had already materialized during a period when these countries combined a small public sector with free-market policies. The welfare state was introduced afterward. That the Nordic countries are so successful is due to an exceptional culture that emphasizes social cohesion, hard work, and individual responsibility.

Today, in contrast, Nordic countries stand out as having high-tax models. Denmark, for example, has the highest tax rate among developed nations. But in 1960, the tax rate in the country was merely 25 percent of GDP, lower than the 27 percent rate in the U.S. at the time. In Sweden, the rate was 29 percent, only slightly higher than in the U.S. In fact, much of Nordic prosperity evolved between the time that a capitalist model was introduced in this part of the world during the late 19th century and the mid-20th century—during the free-market era.

> **The Nordic countries are so successful due to an exceptional culture that emphasizes social cohesion, hard work, and individual responsibility.**

What might come as a surprise to American admirers of the Nordic countries is that high levels of income equality evolved during the same period. Swedish economists Jesper Roine and Daniel Waldenström, for example, explain that "most of the decrease [in income inequality in Sweden] takes place before the expansion of the welfare state and by 1950 Swedish top income shares were already lower than in other countries." A recent paper by economists Anthony Barnes Atkinson and Jakob Egholt Søgaard reaches a similar conclusion for Denmark and Norway.

Cultural norms and mores are hugely important in a country's development—the Scandinavian countries are a prime example. In modern management literature, people from the Nordic countries are described as honest and hard-working. Attitude studies show that they have unusually high levels of societal trust. Historic sources tell us that these attributes were already evident among the Nordic people centuries ago. While some scholars attribute this to the Protestant work ethic, it is likely that climate played an equally important role in creating the Nordic success culture. Nordic farmers owned their land but struggled to survive in the unforgiving climate of Scandinavia. In order to thrive, these homogenous societies developed strict work ethics, healthy lifestyles, and a code of individual responsibility out of necessity. To paraphrase the ancient Persian king Cyrus the Great, hard lands breed hard people.

American admirers of Nordic-style social democracy argue that by copying social-democratic policies, the U.S. will copy Nordic social success. But is this true?

In 1960, well before large welfare states had been created in Nordic countries, Swedes lived 3.2 years longer than Americans, while Norwegians lived 3.8 years longer and Danes 2.4 years longer. Today, after the Nordic countries have introduced universal health care, the difference has shrunk to 2.9 years in Sweden, 2.6 years in Norway, and 1.5 years in Denmark. The differences in life span have actually *shrunk* as Nordic countries moved from a small public sector to a democratic-socialist model with universal health coverage. Moreover, the longest average life spans among Nordic peoples are found in Iceland—the small Nordic cousin that has the most distinctly Nordic culture, but also the most limited welfare system.

It is equally interesting to look at Nordic Americans, a group that combines the Nordic success culture with U.S.-style capitalism. It was mainly the impoverished people in the Nordic countries who sailed across the Atlantic to found new lives. And yet, as I write in my book, Danish Americans today have fully 55 percent higher living standard than Danes. Similarly, Swedish Americans have a 53 percent higher living standard than Swedes. The gap is even greater, 59 percent, between Finnish Americans and Finns. Even though Norwegian Americans lack the oil wealth of Norway, they have a 3 percent higher living standard than their cousins overseas.

Perhaps even more astonishing is that Nordic Americans are more socially successful than their cousins in Scandinavia. They have much lower high-school-dropout rates, much lower unemployment rates, and even slightly lower poverty rates. Similarly, immigrants to the Nordic countries fare worse than those to the U.S. with regard to employment, self-reported health, and the school results of their children.

In short: What the American Left admires about the Nordic countries clearly has less to do with their social-democratic welfare states than with the exceptional culture in these historically Protestant societies.

Currently, Nordic-style democratic socialism is all the rage among Democrat activists as well as with liberal intellectuals and journalists. But in the Nordic countries themselves, this ideal has gradually lost its appeal. Only one of the five Nordic countries, Sweden, currently has a government headed by social democrats. The other four countries have center-right governments. Moreover, the Swedish Social Democrats enjoy weaker popular support today than at any point in modern times. They lead a minority government, as the majority of Swedes either support one of the center-right parties or the anti-immigration party.

During the past few decades, the Nordic countries have gradually been reforming their social systems. Taxes have been cut to stimulate work, public benefits have been limited in order to reduce welfare dependency, pension savings have been partially privatized, for-profit forces have been allowed in the welfare sector, and state monopolies have been opened up to the market. In short, the universal-welfare-state model is being liberalized. Even the social-democratic parties themselves realize the need for change.

Curiously, the American admirers of Nordic-style democratic socialism pay no heed to any of these facts. For them, the Nordic countries serve as a Shangri-La, a promised land reachable through generous welfare policies, high taxes, government redistribution, and a massively expanded public sector. Never mind that a closer look shows that these policies are not what explain the success of Nordic societies, and that the Nordic people themselves are becoming less enthusiastic about democratic socialism. Unfortunately, the American Left is more interested in the Nordic myth than a nuanced view of the actual benefits—and drawbacks—of democratic socialism.

Print Citations

CMS: Sanandaji, Nima. "The Nordic Democratic-Socialist Myth." In *The Reference Shelf: Democracy Evolving,* edited by Micah L. Issitt, 151-154. Amenia, NY: Grey House Publishing, 2019.

MLA: Sanandaji, Nima. "The Nordic Democratic-Socialist Myth." *The Reference Shelf: Democracy Evolving,* edited by Micah L. Issitt, Grey Housing Publishing, 2019, pp. 151-154.

APA: Sanandaji, N. (2019). The Nordic democratic-socialist myth. In Micah L. Issitt (Ed.), *The reference shelf: Democracy evolving* (pp. 151-154). Amenia, NY: Grey Housing Publishing.

Are Millennials Giving Up on Democracy?

By Neil Howe

Forbes, October 31, 2017

Earlier this month, 31-year-old wunderkind Sebastian Kurz was elected as Austria's new chancellor. Kurz—who ran on a populist, anti-immigration platform—is just the latest anti-establishment candidate worldwide to benefit from young people's waning interest in liberal democracy, centrist candidates, and civic process.

Kurz's victory points to an ongoing global youth insurgency that has boosted parties and candidates at the political extremes. In last year's Austrian presidential elections, fully 42% of voters under age 30 checked the box for far-right candidate Norbert Hofer, a prelude to Kurz's victory. In September, Germany's AfD party got a push from younger voters and became the first far-right party in half a century to earn a spot in parliament. And although Emmanuel Macron scored a big victory for the French moderates earlier this year, he was the third choice among the country's youngest voters, who preferred (on the first round) either the far-left Marxist Jean-Luc Mélenchon or the far-right nationalist Marine Le Pen.

Further east, Japan's Shinzo Abe, China's Xi Jinping, India's Narendra Modi, and the Philippines' Rodrigo Duterte all promote socially conservative, ethnically majoritarian, and country-first policies—and, in a reversal from earlier post-war decades, the biggest supporters of such leaders are the young, not the old.

Media commentators offer confusing accounts of this global Millennial trend. Sometimes they explain it as a move leftward (while pointing to Bernie Sanders in America or Jeremy Corbyn in the U.K.), and other times as a move rightward (while pointing at northern Europe or Asia). What unifies Millennials globally, however, is less conventional partisanship than a shift away from the liberal and democratic center. What's more, their goal is unlike that of their own (Boomer and Xer) parents in their youth. They don't want to trash the system and free the individual. They want to rebuild and strengthen the system so it can protect and care for the individual.

Millennial support for populist and authoritarian candidates conforms to several recent studies showing widespread youth disaffection with the whole idea of democracy. Only about 30% of Americans born in the 1980s think it's "essential" to live in a democracy. That's compared to 75% of Americans born in the 1930s. (Australia, New Zealand, Sweden, and Britain reported similar gaps.) In another study of European Millennials, only 32% selected democracy as one of their top five most important social values. And the share of young people who consider democracy a "bad" or "very bad" way to run the United States is growing, according to the World Values Survey.

Millennials are increasingly open to non-democratic forms of government. In 2011, nearly half agreed that it would be a good idea to have "a strong leader" as opposed to "parliament and elections," compared to less than 30% of Boomers and Silent. Similarly, 81% of Millennials think a military takeover would be justified if the government were failing, up from 57% among older Americans. Millennials are also far more likely than older Americans to view socialism favorably, according to Gallup and Pew Research Center.

To be sure, Millennials have joined older generations in distrusting government: Just 27% of U.S. 18- to 29-year-olds trust government to do what's right "always/ most of the time." Yet the youth decline has been shallower than that of older generations. Today, in fact, Millennials report higher levels of trust, higher expectations for services, and less anger at the system than older generations. And what really sets Millennials apart is their expectation and optimism that big institutions *can* be made to work—even if this requires voting in a heavy-handed populist on the left or right.

Why are young people so disillusioned with liberal democracy? Across Europe, high youth unemployment rates (ranging from 15% to 48%) and dismal economic prospects have convinced many that the system simply isn't working, and that new blood is needed to upend the establishment. Fringe parties have taken hold most strongly among youth in countries who feel betrayed by the EU. American Millennials, meanwhile, are fed up with a government they see as gridlocked, corrupt, and unable to solve problems.

> **What really sets Millennials apart is their expectation and optimism that big institutions can be made to work.**

Millennials' skepticism of democracy is in part shaped by their location in history. As political scientists Yascha Mounk and Roberto Stefan Foa point out in the *Washington Post*, Millennials' openness to illiberal alternatives may reflect the fact they "lack the direct experience of living under, or fighting against, authoritarian regimes like fascism or communism."

It's also rooted in a different perception of the future. The young are much more concerned than the old if leaders don't ensure their economic security and prosperity for the long term. Democratic pluralism and neoliberal markets have worked very well to tip power to the old and reward the past—and not so well to help the aspiring young. Global Millennials are much more positive than older generations about Xi Jinping and the new China: They are more impressed by Xi's ability to set clear national priorities and invest hugely in the future, and less bothered by his habit of crushing dissent.

Keep in mind that Millennials tend to seek order (and less conflict) in all areas of their lives. Faced with an abundance of choices and a lack of economic security, they are looking for employers who take care of them *in loco parentis*, all-inclusive retail "deals" that eliminate risk, and brands that take out the guesswork. A one-size-fits-all authority who makes choices for them seems like a great way to go. Single payer health care? Sure, why not?

To be sure, these figures don't mean that Millennials are clamoring for a dictator to take over. Although fewer consider democracy "essential" (i.e., a 10 on a 10-point scale), young people in most countries still, on average, assign it a positive value (around 7 or 8). But their increased attraction to populist authoritarians reveals deep trouble for the moderate center. Young people's thirst for stronger governance may not alone trigger a revolution—but it may lay the groundwork for older radicals who need their support.

Print Citations

CMS: Howe, Neil. "Are Millennials Giving Up on Democracy?" In *The Reference Shelf: Democracy Evolving*, edited by Micah L. Issitt, 155-157. Amenia, NY: Grey House Publishing, 2019.

MLA: Howe, Neil. "Are Millennials Giving Up on Democracy?" *The Reference Shelf: Democracy Evolving*, edited by Micah L. Issitt, Grey Housing Publishing, 2019, pp. 155-157.

APA: Howe, N. (2019). Are millennials giving up on democracy? In Micah L. Issitt (Ed.), *The reference shelf: Democracy evolving* (pp. 155-157). Amenia, NY: Grey Housing Publishing.

On the Sidelines of Democracy: Exploring Why So Many Americans Don't Vote

By Asma Khalid, Don Gonyea, and Leila Fadel
NPR, September 10, 2018

Just in the past few months, elections in the U.S. have been decided by hundreds of votes.

The 2016 presidential election tilted to Donald Trump with fewer than 80,000 votes across three states, with a dramatic impact on the country. Yet, only about 6 in 10 eligible voters cast ballots in 2016.

Among the other 4 in 10 who did not vote was Megan Davis. The 31-year-old massage therapist in Rhode Island never votes, and she's proud of her record.

"I feel like my voice doesn't matter," she said on a recent evening at a park in East Providence, R.I. "People who suck still are in office, so it doesn't make a difference."

Davis might sound contrarian, but she's not. Although these days more Americans say they're enthusiastic about voting in a midterm election than at any point in the last two decades, come Election Day, nonvoters like Davis will still probably be the norm. For every 10 adults eligible to vote, only about four cast a ballot in the 2010 and 2014 midterm elections.

You have to go back to the turn of the 20th century to find a midterm election when a solid majority of people voted (of course, back then, the right to vote was far more limited, so the eligible voting pool was smaller, more male and more white).

Every election cycle there's a lot of attention on *who* voted and why. But there's another important question: *Who* is not voting—and what impact does that have?

The wealthy tend to vote more frequently. Nonvoters are more likely to be poor, young, Hispanic or Asian-American. Some research also indicates they're more likely to align with the Democratic Party.

It's debatable whether election results would be different if the entire population voted, but voting determines more than which candidate wins or loses. It ultimately influences which policies elected officials enact and whose interests candidates ignore and acknowledge.

"The one consistent finding from 1972 up through 2008 and in subsequent elections are that voters and nonvoters have different preferences on economic policies," said Jan Leighley, co-author with Jonathan Nagler of the book *Who Votes Now? Demographics, Issues, Inequality, and Turnout in the United States.*

Her research found that nonvoters are more likely, for example, to support a redistribution of wealth, housing bailouts and expanded social safety net programs.

Hundreds of thousands of nonvoters want to vote, but can't.

In 2016, 4 percent of registered voters did not vote because of "registration problems," according to a Pew Research Center analysis of Census Bureau data. Many would-be voters face a range of barriers: voter ID laws, registration difficulty or criminal records. An estimated 10 percent of adults in Florida, for example, can't vote because of a felony conviction.

Some people who want to vote but can't have been removed from the voting rolls. Across the country, the rate at which people are being purged from the voting rolls, a process historically intended to keep records updated, has increased substantially compared to a decade ago, according to a report from the Brennan Center published this summer. The analysis found 4 million more people were purged between 2014 and 2016 than in the equivalent period between 2006 and 2008.

Legal obstacles are an important part of the nonvoter story, but there are many millions of Americans who can vote and yet choose not to. Their reasons are vast: Some are apathetic or too busy. Others don't like their choices, they don't think their vote matters, they think the system is corrupt, or they don't think they know enough to vote.

NPR traveled to four states where different factors affect why people aren't voting at high levels—age, income, education level, and habits.

Las Vegas: The Young and Disengaged

Shelby Mabis, a stocky blonde Marine corps veteran, remembers taking a government class in high school, but said he didn't learn anything about voting.

"From what all I know about voting is you show up to a poll place and you vote, but I don't know what I need to bring. I don't even know what happens during there," said Mabis, 23, outside of his mandatory political science class at a community college in North Las Vegas. And so he's never voted before.

Mabis is not unusual. There's a high density of people in his area who don't vote, as in many places.

"Whenever young people are surveyed, there is a significant lack of knowledge about how exactly the government works, and, therefore, how their vote actually matters," said Kei Kawashima-Ginsberg, the director of CIRCLE, an initiative at Tufts University that studies youth civic and political participation. She recently conducted a survey of working-class youth, and found that nearly 20 percent of young people said they don't think they know enough to be able to vote.

Her research has found that a majority of young people don't think voting is an effective way to change society. They also have major misconceptions about voting. Some think getting a citation for driving under the influence meant they could no longer vote.

But for Mabis, not voting is not just about education—it's about location.

"Right now, being away from home, I don't feel connected to the political system here at all," he said, referring to Nevada. "Since I'm not from here, I really feel like this isn't my home."

Mabis grew up in Missouri, and that's where he registered to vote. But he said it's not easy to stay connected to Missouri politics.

Analysts say this is common—young people are more often transient and so they often feel less invested in local elections.

Youth turnout nationwide for midterms is around 20 percent. For older adults, it's closer to 50 percent. When you look at who votes frequently over many years, the numbers look even starker.

In over a dozen interviews, NPR heard similar reasons from young nonvoters for why they don't participate in politics: they don't feel their vote matters, they don't care, they're busy, or they don't feel like they know enough to vote.

But in some cases, they're also particularly eager to choose individual candidates instead of a party label. In 2016, many said they felt uninspired by both Hillary Clinton and Donald Trump.

So, like Jonas Rand, they didn't vote for president.

"I don't believe it is actually effective to vote as a main method of accomplishing political change," said Rand, a senior who studies anthropology at the University of Nevada, Las Vegas.

Rand follows the news closely, he considers himself a political activist, but he's not a fan of the current two-party political system.

"The system itself is stacked against the citizenry," he said.

He thinks Trump is a "fascist," but still he doesn't see how voting for Clinton would have changed anything, pointing out that Nevada's votes in the Electoral College went for Clinton anyhow.

But if young people don't vote, they're less likely to be targeted by political campaigns. And that worries community activist Francisco Morales.

"It's no coincidence that politicians care a lot about Medicare and Social Security. Seniors vote all the time," said Morales, state director for the Center for Community Change Action.

But, he says, issues that millennials care about, such as student debt, are often overlooked "because politicians are not afraid of our voting bloc."

West Virginia: The Class Divide

McDowell County, W.Va., is the county with the lowest voter turnout in a state that had one of the lowest turnout rates in the country in 2016.

In Welch, W.Va., the county seat, median household income hovers around $25,000 a year. Sixty one percent of registered voters in McDowell County are nonvoters, people who have voted zero or one time in the last eight elections, according to a review of data from L2, a nonpartisan voter file vendor.

Tammy Lester, a 42-year-old fast food worker in McDowell County, W.Va., can't remember the last time she voted.

"We vote these people in and they don't help McDowell County," she said, as she walked along the deserted streets in the rundown downtown with her daughter. "There's nothing ... there's no jobs when our kids graduate, they have to leave."

Beyond a movie theater, a small pharmacy, and a couple of county offices, most of the storefronts are closed. A couple of years ago, the closest Walmart shut down, and now there's hardly anywhere locals can buy fresh produce.

Lester said politicians always ignore her county. "We are last on everything," she said.

"What good does it do, though, when they'll promise you anything and then it's a lie," she asked rhetorically.

Lester, like many nonvoters, never went to college. She stopped going to school in eighth grade. Research has shown the biggest and most persistent difference between who votes and who doesn't is education and economics. Class is a more accurate predictor of voting behavior than race, ethnicity, gender or any other demographic factor, according to Jan Leighley. Leighley writes

> **Across the country, the rate at which people are being purged from the voting rolls has increased substantially compared to a decade ago.**

in her book *Who Votes Now?* that nearly 80 percent of high-income earners vote, compared to barely 50 percent of low-income Americans.

"I just don't think my vote matters," said Josh Mullins, as he pushed a stroller along the street in McDowell County.

The last time Mullins, a 33-year-old unemployed former restaurant worker, remembers voting was in 2004 for Democratic presidential nominee John Kerry. Nowadays, he sees no point, saying the system overrules what people want.

"Hillary [Clinton] won the popular vote and we still have Trump for president," he said. "To me it says ... it was just the [Electoral College] that put Trump in office." Voters in each state determined the Electoral College outcome.

Another major reason people say they don't vote is the time and effort taken away from other priorities.

"They're working several jobs, they're low-income, they're low-education, they're younger and they decide the costs are too high for them," explained Michael McDonald, a political scientist at the University of Florida who tracks turnout at the U.S. Elections Project. "They decide they've got a lot of other things going on in their lives."

El Paso, Texas: Low Latino Turnout

At the Bowie Bakery, a popular institution in El Paso's Segundo Barrio, or second ward, Christina Rodriguez examined the glass cases filled with Mexican sweet breads, tres leches cakes, cupcakes, cookies and pastries. She ordered a batch of cookies for her 15-year-old's quinceañera and made her way to the door.

Rodriguez, a 38-year-old single, working mom, is always on the go. It's why, she says, she doesn't vote.

"I don't even know who's running,'" she said, laughing with a bit of embarrassment. "I should look into it, but, honestly, I haven't given it more than a thought."

She doesn't have time, she said, to look up the candidates, research their platforms and head to the polls.

"I'd rather not show up and do an uneducated guess," she said. "I don't want to make a mistake."

Growing up, her parents never voted either. Voting, she said, wasn't part of the culture in this border city where over 80 percent of residents identify as Latino.

"Voting is often taught and it may take a couple generations to become a habit," said Lisa Wise, the elections administrator in El Paso.

Some immigrant families are still unfamiliar with voting. Experts suggest this might also explain why Asian-American voter participation is low, despite high education levels. The adult Asian-American population is largely still foreign-born.

"I do what I do to make my life better," said Rodriguez. "I don't depend on (politicians) to change things for me."

But analysts say low Latino turnout in Texas isn't occurring in a vacuum. Texas has long been home to one of the worst voter turnout rates in the country; 51.6 percent of Texans voted in 2016.

Research has shown that competition energizes the electorate, and Texas is largely not seen as a competitive state, particularly in presidential years. Locals say they have a joke in El Paso that the only time a major presidential candidate passes through the city is when he's driving to New Mexico.

"Texas has not had the swing state machine that we've seen in other places around the country," said Mindy Romero, director of the California Civic Engagement Project at the USC Sol Price School of Public Policy. "There aren't those resources, money, and investment coming into the state to get every voter." This is also an issue in California, the state with the largest Latino population.

Broad political apathy seeps into local and statewide elections, too. At the Bowie Bakery in El Paso, most customers didn't know that their native son, Beto O'Rourke, is running in a closely watched Senate race against Republican incumbent Ted Cruz. They didn't know that if O'Rourke wins he would be the first Democratic senator elected from Texas in a quarter century.

It also doesn't help engage voters that El Paso has had a history of corrupt elected officials.

Texas is undoubtedly one of the highest nonvoting states in the country, but poor Latino turnout goes far beyond the borders of Texas.

More than half of eligible Latinos nationally don't vote. In the last presidential election, Latinos represented 12 percent of eligible voters nationwide, but only 9 percent of the overall electorate on Election Day.

Many analysts predicted that Donald Trump's offensive rhetoric about Latinos would mobilize records numbers of Latino voters in 2016, but turnout remained relatively even with 2012.

"You may be upset about somebody like Donald Trump and what you're hearing," said Romero. "But if you don't see how or why ... politicians and the political landscape matters for you ... you don't think you have agency,"

Romero points to two main reasons so many Latinos are nonvoters: the disconnect they feel with the political process and the anemic investment in outreach.

But Romero doesn't blame the Latino community, she and Leighley both point out that candidates rarely try to reach new voters.

"This idyllic notion that campaigns are out there to get everyone to vote is simply not true," said Leighley. "They need one more vote than their opponent, they will go to people based on those voter files that they know have voted before and they focus on them."

It's more expensive and time consuming to chase down infrequent voters.

Print Citations

CMS: Khalid, Asma, Gonyea, Don, and Leila Fadel. "On the Sidelines of Democracy: Exploring Why So Many Americans Don't Vote." In *The Reference Shelf: Democracy Evolving,* edited by Micah L. Issitt, 158-163. Amenia, NY: Grey House Publishing, 2019.

MLA: Khalid, Asma, Gonyea, Don, and Leila Fadel. "On the Sidelines of Democracy: Exploring Why So Many Americans Don't Vote." *The Reference Shelf: Democracy Evolving,* edited by Micah L. Issitt, Grey Housing Publishing, 2019, pp. 158-163.

APA: Khalid, A., Gonyea, D., & Fadel, L. (2019). On the sidelines of democracy: Exploring why so many Americans don't vote. (2019). In Micah L. Issitt (Ed.), *The reference shelf: Democracy evolving* (pp. 158-163). Amenia, NY: Grey Housing Publishing.

Bibliography

Abramowitz, Michael J. and Wendell L. Willkie II. "We Looked at the State of Democracy around the World, and the Results Are Grim." *The Washington Post.* Jan 17, 2018. Retrieved from https://www.washingtonpost.com/news/democracy-post/wp/2018/01/17/we-looked-at-the-state-of-democracy-around-the-world-and-the-results-are-grim/?utm_term=.b71e1af30fef.

Amadeo, Kimberly. "Income Inequality in America." *The Balance.* Nov 7, 2018. Retrieved from https://www.thebalance.com/income-inequality-in-america-3306190.

Beichman, Arnold. "Who Won the Cold War?" *Hoover Institution.* Jul 2, 2001. Retrieved from https://www.hoover.org/research/who-won-cold-war.

Brands, Hal. "China's Master Plan: Exporting an Ideology." *Bloomberg.* Jun 11, 2018. Retrieved from https://www.bloomberg.com/opinion/articles/2018-06-11/china-s-master-plan-exporting-an-ideology.

Bump, Philip. "The President Was Never Intended to Be the Most Powerful Part of Government." *The Washington Post.* Feb 13, 2017. Retrieved from https://www.washingtonpost.com/news/politics/wp/2017/02/13/the-president-was-never-intended-to-be-the-most-powerful-part-of-government/?noredirect=on&utm_term=.2b1f5f74e44e.

Chait, Jonathan. "Conservatives Can't Distinguish Between Democratic Reform and Authoritarianism." *New York.* Mar 29, 2019. Retrieved from http://nymag.com/intelligencer/2019/03/trump-authoritarian-electoral-college-popular-vote-democracy.html.

Crowson, H.M, Thoma, S.J., and Hestevold, N. "Is Political Conservatism Synonymous with Authoritarianism? *Journal of Social Psychology.* 2005. Oct, Vol. 145, No. 5, 571-92.

"Democracy in Retreat." *Freedom House.* Freedom in the World 2019. Retrieved from https://freedomhouse.org/report/freedom-world/freedom-world-2019/democracy-in-retreat.

Desilver, Drew. "U.S. Trails Most Developed Countries in Voter Turnout." *Pew Research Center.* May 21, 2018. Retrieved from https://www.pewresearch.org/fact-tank/2018/05/21/u-s-voter-turnout-trails-most-developed-countries/.

Geltzer, Joshua. "America's Problem Isn't Too Little Democracy: It's Too Much." *Politico Magazine.* June 26, 2018. Retrieved from https://www.politico.com/magazine/story/2018/06/26/america-democracy-trump-russia-2016-218894.

Gonzales, Richard. "5 Questions About DACA Answered." *NPR.* Sep 5, 2017. Retrieved from https://www.npr.org/2017/09/05/548754723/5-things-you-should-know-about-daca.

Gopal, Anand. "How the US Created the Afghan War—and Then Lost It." *The Nation*. Apr 29, 2014. Retrieved from https://www.thenation.com/article/how-us-created-afghan-war-and-then-lost-it/.

Gould, Elise. "Decades of Rising Economic Inequality in the U.S." *EPI*. Economic Policy Institute. Mar 27, 2019. Retrieved from https://www.epi.org/publication/decades-of-rising-economic-inequality-in-the-u-s-testimony-before-the-u-s-house-of-representatives-ways-and-means-committee/.

Haltiwanger, John. "Here's the Difference between a 'Socialist' and a 'Democratic Socialist'." *Business Insider*. Feb 25, 2019. Retrieved from https://www.businessinsider.com/difference-between-socialist-and-democratic-socialist-2018-6.

Huyssen, David. "We Won't Get Out of the Second Gilded Age the Way We Got Out of the First." *Vox*. Apr 1, 2019. Retrieved from https://www.vox.com/first-person/2019/4/1/18286084/gilded-age-income-inequality-robber-baron.

"Income Inequality." *Pew Research Center*. May 7, 2019. Retrieved from https://www.pewresearch.org/topics/income-inequality/.

Illing, Sean. "White Identity Politics Is about More than Racism." *Vox*. Apr 27, 2019. Retrieved from https://www.vox.com/2019/4/26/18306125/white-identity-politics-trump-racism-ashley-jardina.

Jacobson, Louis. "Donald Trump's Pants on Fire Claim about 'Treason'." *Politifact*. Feb 6, 2018. Retrieved from https://www.politifact.com/truth-o-meter/statements/2018/feb/06/donald-trump/donald-trumps-pants-fire-claim-about-treason/.

Kurlantzick, Joshua. "The State of Global Democracy Today Is Even Worse Than It Looks: V-Demo's New Democracy Research." *Council on Foreign Relations*. Apr 3, 2019. Retrieved from https://www.cfr.org/blog/state-global-democracy-today-even-worse-it-looks-v-dems-new-democracy-research.

Lipset, Seymour Martin and Gary Marks. *It Didn't Happen Here: Why Socialism Failed in the United States*. New York: W.W. Norton & Company, 2000.

Longley, Robert. "Learn about Direct Democracy and Its Pros and Cons." *Thought Co*. Jan 21, 2019. Retrieved from https://www.thoughtco.com/what-is-direct-democracy-3322038.

Lopez, German. "The Battle over Identity Politics, Explained." *Vox*. Aug 17, 2017. Retrieved from https://www.vox.com/identities/2016/12/2/13718770/identity-politics.

Lucci, Micol. "This Is How Switzerland's Direct Democracy Works." *We Forum*. We Forum. Jul 31 2017. Retrieved from https://www.weforum.org/agenda/2017/07/switzerland-direct-democracy-explained/.

Mohdin, Aamna. "Fewer Than Half of Americans Are 'Extremely Proud' of Their Country." *QZ*. Jul 4, 2018. Retrieved from https://qz.com/1321228/fewer-than-half-of-americans-are-extremely-proud-of-their-country-for-the-first-time-in-18-years-gallup/.

Mounk, Yascha. "America Is Not a Democracy." *The Atlantic*. March 2018. Retrieved from https://www.theatlantic.com/magazine/archive/2018/03/america-is-not-a-democracy/550931/.

"Public Trust in Government: 1958-2019." *Pew Research Center*. Apr 11, 2019. Retrieved from https://www.people-press.org/2019/04/11/public-trust-in-government-1958-2019/.

"Read Sen. Jeff Flake's Speech Criticizing Trump." *CNN*. Jan 17, 2018. Retrieved from https://www.cnn.com/2018/01/17/politics/jeff-flake-speech/index.html.

Rothman, Lily. "How American Inequality in the Gilded Age Compares to Today." *Time*. Feb 5, 2018. Retrieved from http://time.com/5122375/american-inequality-gilded-age/.

Rudd, Kevin. "The Rise of Authoritarian Capitalism." *The New York Times*. Sep 16, 2018. Retrieved from https://www.nytimes.com/2018/09/16/opinion/politics/kevin-rudd-authoritarian-capitalism.html.

Singal, Jesse. "How Social Science Might Be Misunderstanding Conservatives." *New York*. Jul 15, 2018. Retrieved from http://nymag.com/intelligencer/2018/07/how-social-science-might-be-misunderstanding-conservatives.html.

Stephan, Maria J. and Timothy Snyder. "Authoritarianism Is Making a Comeback: Here's the Time-Tested Way to Defeat It." *The Guardian*. Jun 20, 2017. Retrieved from https://www.theguardian.com/commentisfree/2017/jun/20/authoritarianism-trump-resistance-defeat.

Stern, Mark Joseph. "The New Trove of Secret Gerrymandering Files Will Be a Nightmare for the GOP." *Slate*. May 31, 2019. Retrieved from https://slate.com/news-and-politics/2019/05/thomas-hofeller-secret-gerrymandering-files-north-carolina.html.

Stiglitz, Joseph E. "A 'Democratic Socialist' Agenda Is Appealing: No Wonder Trump Attacks It." *The Washington Post*. May 8, 2019. Retrieved from https://www.washingtonpost.com/opinions/a-democratic-socialist-agenda-is-appealing-no-wonder-trump-attacks-it/2019/05/08/f3db9e42-71a2-11e9-9eb4-0828f5389013_story.html?utm_term=.3cce33a1d2de.

Suedfeld, Peter. "Authoritarian Thinking, Groupthink, and Decision-Making Under Stress: Are Simple Decisions Always Worse?" *American Psychological Association*. August 1986.

Taylor, Jessica. "Republicans and Democrats Don't Agree, or Like Each Other—And It's Worse Than Ever." *NPR*. Oct 5, 2017. Retrieved from https://www.npr.org/2017/10/05/555685136/republicans-and-democrats-dont-agree-dont-like-each-other-and-its-worst-than-eve.

Todd, Chuck, Murray, Mark, and Carrie Dann. "Russian Interference Is the Red Flag from Mueller That Everyone Is Missing." *NBC News*. May 30, 2019. Retrieved from https://www.nbcnews.com/politics/meet-the-press/russian-interference-red-flag-mueller-everyone-missing-n1011866.

Volokh, Eugene. "The United States Is Both a 'Republic' and a 'Democracy' —Because 'Democracy' Is Like 'Cash'." *The Washington Post*. Nov 14, 2016. Retrieved from https://www.washingtonpost.com/news/volokh-conspiracy/wp/2016/11/14/the-united-states-is-both-a-republic-and-a-democracy-because-democracy-is-like-cash/?noredirect=on&utm_term=.5be8dad54035.

Waxman, Olivia B. "Socialism Was Once America's Political Taboo: Now, Democratic Socialism Is a Viable Platform. Here's What to Know." *Time*. Oct 24, 2018. Retrieved from http://time.com/5422714/what-is-democratic-socialism/.

Westad, Odd Arne. "The Cold War and America's Delusion of Victory." *The New York Times*. Aug 28, 2017. Retrieved from https://www.nytimes.com/2017/08/28/opinion/cold-war-american-soviet-victory.html.

Wheeler, Marcy. "What Mueller's Reminder about Russian Interference Really Meant." *The Washington Post*. May 30, 2019. https://www.washingtonpost.com/outlook/2019/05/30/what-muellers-reminder-about-russian-interference-really-meant/?noredirect=on&utm_term=.03ea5acc0b33.

"Who We Are & What We Do." *DSA*. Democratic Socialists of America. Retrieved from https://www.dsausa.org.

Wike, Richard, Simmons, Katie, Stokes, Bruce, and Janell Fetterolf. "Democracy Widely Supported, Little Backing for Rule by Strong Leader or Military." *Pew Research Center*. Oct 16, 2017. Retrieved from https://www.pewresearch.org/global/2017/10/16/democracy-widely-supported-little-backing-for-rule-by-strong-leader-or-military/.

Williams, Armstrong. "America's Unique Democracy." *Townhall*. Jul 12, 2011. Retrieved from https://townhall.com/columnists/armstrongwilliams/2011/07/12/americas-unique-democracy-n1376836.

Wood, Gordon S. "The Origins of American Democracy, or How the People Became Judges in Their Own Causes, The Sixty-Ninth Cleveland-Marshall Fund Lecture." *Cleveland State Law Review*. 1999. Retrieved from https://engagedscholarship.csuohio.edu/cgi/viewcontent.cgi?referer=https://www.google.com/&httpsredir=1&article=1487&context=clevstlrev.

Yuen Yuen Ang. "Autocracy with Chinese Characteristics." *Foreign Affairs*. May/June 2018. Retrieved from https://www.foreignaffairs.com/articles/asia/2018-04-16/autocracy-chinese-characteristics.

Websites

Center for International Private Enterprise (CIPE)

www.cipe.org

The Center for International Private Enterprise is a suborganization within the larger National Endowment for Democracy and seeks to promote democratic capitalism around the world. The organization was founded in the 1980s, under the Reagan Administration, and provides research and economic assistance to support capitalism and free-market initiatives. CIPE works closely with the U.S. Chamber of Commerce and receives federal funding for some of the organization's programs.

Democracy for America (DFA)

www.democracyforamerica.com

Democracy for America (DFA) is a progressive political action committee that supports progressive candidates for U.S. office. The organization promotes itself as a pro-democratic activist organization and participated in a number of programs intended to promote American democratic politics, and has more than a million members in the United States and abroad. Key issues for DFA activists including economic inequality, reproductive rights, affirmative action, and promoting the inclusion of LGBTQ and people of color in American politics.

Democratic Socialists of America

www.dsusa.org

DSUSA is the largest democratic socialist organization in the United States and was founded in 1982 from a merger of two earlier organizations, the Democratic Socialist Organizing Committee (DSOC) and the New American Movement (NAM), established in the 1970s. DSUSA advocates for the adoption of social reform policies like universal healthcare, universal higher education, and expanded programs for the redistribution of wealth. The DSUSA website provides information on the history of democratic socialism and the aims of the movement with regard to advocating within the United States.

Freedom House

www.freedomhouse.org

Freedom House is a U.S.-based nongovernmental organization (NGO) that is focused on researching and promoting democratic government and human rights. Freedom House is known for the organization's annual "Freedom in the World" report in which the organization utilizes a set of criteria to evaluate the state of global democratic governments. Freedom House also published analyses of international press freedom and human rights. Freedom House is one of America's oldest and most prestigious progressive democratic organizations and was founded in 1941 by famous democratic theorist Wendell Willkie and former First Lady Eleanor Roosevelt.

Green Party

www.gp.org

The Green Party is an American political party and one of the nation's largest and most visible alternatives to the Democratic and Republican Parties. The Green Party focuses on environmental initiatives and social welfare reform. Members of the Green Party were instrumental in crafting proposals for the Green New Deal a series of progressive initiatives meant to address income inequality and environmental protection towards the goal of addressing American's ongoing climate crisis. Though the Green Party has not managed to achieve mainstream success at the highest levels of federal politics, the party has been instrumental in shaping the evolving Democratic Party platform.

Indivisible

www.indivisible.org

Indivisible is an American progressive movement and one of a host of new progressive organizations that emerged in the wake of Donald Trump's election and representing the perception of an emerging authoritarian threat to American society. The organization trains and supports activists resisting aspects of the Trump administration agenda seen as anti-democratic or anti-progressive and has been influential in promoting young progressive candidates for a number of U.S. political offices.

National Endowment for Democracy (NED)

www.ned.org

The National Endowment for Democracy is a private, nonprofit organization founded in the United States with the goal of promoting democratic development abroad. NED publishes the *Journal of Democracy* and also supports a number of associated and more focused organizations including the International Forum for Democratic Studies and the World Movement for Democracy. The National Endowment for Democracy is generally conservative and representative of Reagan-era Republican Party policies that sought to promote democracy as part of the broader Cold War ideological competition and characteristic U.S. fear of non-capitalism philosophy.

Pew Research Center
www.pew.org

Pew Research Center in a nonprofit U.S.-based think tank and research organization that supports and creates research studies measuring public opinion on a wide variety of topics. Pew Research studies frequently address issues involving aspects of American democracy, including public opinion on the state of the government, the economy, and other issues relevant to America's democratic institutions and public perception.

U.S. Bureau of Democracy, Human Rights, and Labor
www.state.gov

The U.S. Bureau of Democracy, Human Rights, and Labor (DRL) is a branch of the U.S. Department of State charged with promoting American democracy around the world and also with organizing and promoting U.S. human rights policies and labor issues. The DRL produces annual reports and supports research regarding the state of American democracy in the United States and around the world.

Index